Data Journalism and the Regeneration of News

Data Journalism and the Regeneration of News traces the emergence of data journalism through a scholarly lens. It reveals the growth of data journalism as a subspecialty, cultivated and sustained by an increasing number of professional identities, tools and technologies, educational opportunities and new forms of collaboration and computational thinking.

The authors base their analysis on five years of in-depth field research, largely in Canada, an example of a mature media system. The book identifies how data journalism's development is partly due to it being at the center of multiple crises and shocks to journalism, including digitalization, acute mis- and dis-information concerns and increasingly participatory audiences. It highlights how data journalists, particularly in well-resourced newsrooms, are able to address issues of trust and credibility to advance their professional interests. These journalists are operating as institutional entrepreneurs in a field still responding to the disruption effects of digitalization more than 20 years ago.

By exploring the ways in which data journalists are strategically working to modernize the way journalists talk about methods and maintain journalism authority, *Data Journalism and the Regeneration of News* introduces an important new dimension to the study of digital journalism for researchers, students and educators.

Alfred Hermida, PhD, is an award-winning author, media scholar and digital news pioneer. A journalism professor at the University of British Columbia, co-founder and board member of The Conversation Canada, and formerly a BBC journalist, his research explores media innovation, social media and data journalism.

Mary Lynn Young, PhD, is a journalism professor at the University of British Columbia, and co-founder and board member of The Conversation Canada. Formerly a journalist and academic administrator, her research interests include gender, newsroom sociology, data journalism, media start-ups and representations of crime.

Disruptions: Studies in Digital Journalism

Series editor: Bob Franklin

Disruptions refers to the radical changes provoked by the affordances of digital technologies that occur at a pace and on a scale that disrupts settled understandings and traditional ways of creating value, interacting and communicating both socially and professionally. The consequences for digital journalism involve far reaching changes to business models, professional practices, roles, ethics, products and even challenges to the accepted definitions and understandings of journalism. For Digital Journalism Studies, the field of academic inquiry which explores and examines digital journalism, disruption results in paradigmatic and tectonic shifts in scholarly concerns. It prompts reconsideration of research methods, theoretical analyses and responses (oppositional and consensual) to such changes, which have been described as being akin to "a moment of mind blowing uncertainty."

Routledge's new book series, ***Disruptions: Studies in Digital Journalism***, seeks to capture, examine and analyze these moments of exciting and explosive professional and scholarly innovation which characterize developments in the day-to-day practice of journalism in an age of digital media, and which are articulated in the newly emerging academic discipline of Digital Journalism Studies.

Social Media Livestreaming
Claudette G. Artwick

Citizen Journalism: Practices, Propaganda, Pedagogy
Melissa Wall

Data Journalism and the Regeneration of News
Alfred Hermida and Mary Lynn Young

A Short History of Disruptive Journalism Technologies: 1960–1990
Will Mari

www.routledge.com/Disruptions/book-series/DISRUPTDIGJOUR

Data Journalism and the Regeneration of News

Alfred Hermida and Mary Lynn Young

Routledge
Taylor & Francis Group
LONDON AND NEW YORK

First published 2019
by Routledge
2 Park Square, Milton Park, Abingdon, Oxon OX14 4RN

and by Routledge
52 Vanderbilt Avenue, New York, NY 10017

Routledge is an imprint of the Taylor & Francis Group, an informa business

British Library Cataloguing-in-Publication Data
A catalogue record for this book is available from the British Library

Library of Congress Cataloging-in-Publication Data
A catalog record for this book has been requested

ISBN: 978-1-138-05893-4 (hbk)
ISBN: 978-1-315-16389-5 (ebk)

Typeset in Times New Roman
by Apex CoVantage, LLC

Contents

Acknowledgments

Thank you to all the journalists who gave up their time to share their expertise and experiences with us. We deeply appreciate their willingness to answer our questions and offer insightful perspectives into their professional worlds.

We are grateful for all of the scholarly interventions and contributions along the way, from a 2016 reading group led by Rasmus Kleis Nielsen for visiting scholars at the Reuters Institute for the Study of Journalism at Oxford University that introduced some of the institutional and organizational literature, to a connection with Tom Lawrence on the board of a media non-profit.

UBC computer science professor Tamara Munzner and journalist Caitlin Havlak kindly shared their syllabi and accepted auditors in their course. Scholars who read drafts of the manuscript and provided invaluable insights include Charles Berret, Candis Callison, Seth Lewis, and of course, we are forever grateful to series editor Bob Franklin for his feedback and support of this project over the years.

We would not be here without the contributions of our research assistants Gen Cruz, Johanna Fulda, Elizabeth Hames and Rithika Shenoy.

We are thankful to the faculty, staff and students at the School of Journalism at the University of British Columbia for a collegial and collaborative environment.

We would like to acknowledge funding support for our research from Graphics, Animation and New Media (GRAND) – Networks of Centres of Excellence – as part of the NEWS and NEWS2 projects.

We are grateful for the continued encouragement and advice of Rachel Nixon and Kirk LaPointe who have shared the journey with us.

Introduction

The night of Thursday May 1, 1997, marked a sea change in British politics as Tony Blair's Labour Party swept to power and ended 18 years of Conservative rule. It was also momentous for U.K. journalism: BBC journalists covered the election not only on radio and TV, but for the first time, online. A dedicated BBC website, Election 1997, published the results in near real-time, with details from across the country. Not surprisingly digital and data came together over a news event central to journalism's role in civic engagement – an election. Compared to previous election coverage, the site enabled voters to drill down into the figures and learn the result for their constituencies as the numbers were coming in near real-time.

Election 1997 predated by several months the launch of the BBC's digital news service, BBC News Online in November 1997 (Webber, 2017). I was one of the journalists assigned to Election 1997 and later BBC News Online, coming from a background in BBC radio and television news. Working alongside developers and designers, we made these first forays into what was a new medium for the long-standing public service broadcaster. At the time, we felt we were charting new ground, going beyond the established practices of BBC radio and television journalism to explore forms of multimedia storytelling, audience interaction and information storage and retrieval. These first few years have been described by staff working at the site as a "'Wild West,' or as a place where they 'operated like pirates' and were 'completely independent and bloody-minded'" (Küng-Shankleman, 2003: p. 7). We had to be as we were trying to innovate in the oldest public broadcaster at the beginning of journalism's digital age. On the one hand, journalism was undergoing digitization, changing from analog to digital bits. But it was also undergoing digitalization, which captures how journalism is restructured by digital communication and media infrastructures (Brennen & Kreiss, 2016).

This introduction offers a personal perspective on the trajectory of the impact of digital on journalism, drawing on my experiences as a founding editor of the BBC News website. It considers experiences and examples from the naissance of online journalism at the public broadcaster as a means to trace possible parallels and divergences with the development of data journalism. Both could be seen to serve as what Fligstein and McAdam deem emergent strategic action fields,

> where actors [who can be individual or collective] interact with knowledge of one another under a set of common understandings about the purposes of the field, the relationships in the field [including who has power and why], and the field's rules.
>
> (2011: p. 3)

For more than 20 years, I have been privileged to participate in the twists and turns of the emergence and evolution of digital journalism, first as a founding news editor at the BBC News website, and then, since 2006, as a scholar-practitioner at the University of British Columbia. Book co-author, Mary Lynn Young, has followed her own trajectory from print to digital and academia, having joined the University of British Columbia in 2000. While I was attracted to the possibilities for new ways of telling stories online, little did I realize in 1997 how far digitalization was going to contribute to the disruption of the relatively consistent state of 20th-century professional journalism (Küng, Leandros, Picard, Schroeder & Van der Wurff, 2008). Two decades on from the first era of online news, the literature in the field has tracked the tensions between continuity and change over norms, practices, identities, structures and orientations with an eye towards technological disruption and its possibilities for the future (Boczkowski, 2004; Domingo, 2008; Singer et al., 2011).

People

The advent of digital opened the door for new actors in the newsroom with different skill sets and attitudes. In 1997, BBC News Online, as the unit was called at the time, launched with a small team of 30 journalists and technologists. For a broadcast organization, this created the new subspeciality of journalist – the journalist producing content for online platforms, alongside those working for radio and television (Usher, 2016). On the news side was a combination of senior and experienced BBC journalists curious about the potential of the Internet, and younger journalists, largely recruited from newspapers. At the time, I had been working at BBC World Television, having come back to London from four years as a BBC correspondent in North Africa and the Middle East. My editor knew about my interest in the multimedia and interactive possibilities presented by digital so I was offered the opportunity to work temporarily on the Election 97 site, and subsequently to move permanently to BBC News Online.

The mix of "old hands" from inside and "new blood" from outside the organization was key to the success of the site. Leading the editorial side as editor-in-chief from launch until 2004 was Mike Smartt, a respected BBC TV correspondent with 20 years of experience at the corporation. As Küng-Shankleman notes, the strategy "brought advantages in that the new journalists were young, fresh and keen" (2003: p. 12). Notably, most of the new blood came from legacy print organizations. It meant they did not come with a broadcast mentality or the prevailing paternalistic attitude towards audiences inherited from the founder of the BBC, Lord Reith. These staff formed a new occupational subgroup at the BBC, the online journalists. Similarly, data journalists have emerged as an occupational subgroup, combining public interest journalism with newer approaches. Both introduce novel forms of work, prompting questions over how they relate to established roles and responsibilities.

Incumbents seek to maintain the status quo in the face of challengers. In the BBC's case, many radio and television journalists were dismissive of the notion that digital editorial work was journalism. At BBC News Online, we were seen as the techies by our counterparts in radio and TV news. As one journalist noted, online "was a nerdy thing that didn't really matter" (quoted in Küng-Shankleman, 2003: p. 7). A seasoned BBC journalist, World Affairs Editor John Simpson, said it sounded "quite nerdy" (BBC News Website, 2004: para.4). For years, one of the ways TV and radio resisted online was by refusing to mention it on air or direct viewers and listeners to the website. The upside was that being ignored by other news platforms proved beneficial in the early days as it "allowed a culture to flourish that was very different from the mainstream BBC way of doing things" (quoted in Küng-Shankleman, 2003: p. 9).

The culture at BBC News Online was fostered through our shared occupational identity as digital journalists navigating change within a revered broadcast organization. We had our own specific professional formation, with our own in-house best practice guidelines and dedicated training workshops. For a year, I held weekly one-day training sessions to introduce new recruits to the notion of the story as a constantly updated digital package of text, visuals, audio, video and links, recognizing that we existed in a busy digital media space where audiences could click away within seconds. At the same time, we had to operate within fundamental BBC journalistic values of accuracy, impartiality, independence, accountability and serving the public interest.

The divisions between emergent and established journalistic identities have been documented in the literature (Barnhurst, 1994; Lowrey, 2002;

Zelizer, 1995), showing how incumbents in print and broadcast have sought to mobilize definitions of journalism to maintain their power. A 1999 study of online journalists found that they tended to see themselves as second-class citizens in the newsroom (Singer, Tharp & Haruta, 1999). Powers (2012) notes that people with computing skills, such as programmers and developers, have a history of being labeled as engaging in non-journalistic forms of work. The idea that digital was subordinate to other media was evident in the evolution of digital journalism in the U.S. in the late 1990s. Powers explains that "online journalists in general and computer programmers in particular were seen as necessary but insufficient forms of emerging work; necessary because of their technical expertise, insufficient because of their lack of journalistic know-how" (2012: p. 33).

Places

The location of a digital or data operation, both physically and organizationally, speaks volumes as it indicates how the governance structure of a unit is considered as internal or external to a field. Space takes on a social meaning not just as a set of boundaries but also as defined by the people working in it (Gieryn, 2000). Discussing the relocation and downsizing of print newsrooms, Usher suggests that "if journalists cannot adjust, and newsrooms remain caught up in reminiscing about the old physical location, they may not look for stories that may be equally compelling and new" (2015: p. 1018). And nostalgia, she suggests, may mean newsrooms falling "behind in thinking about information and their public role as a critical source of news in an urban information ecology" (2015: p. 1018).

At its launch, BBC News Online was very much the outsider at the public broadcaster, both physically and metaphorically. The newsroom was located on the seventh floor of a wing of BBC Television Centre in west London. It was in the same building as the BBC's bi-media news operation but separated by several floors and winding corridors. Not only did the website have its own newsroom, it was out of the sight of the established news operations. The separation spoke to the high degree of autonomy enjoyed by the digital newsroom from its broadcast siblings, which was fundamental in the unit's ability to develop and innovate online. When the BBC started working on plans in 2002 to extend its flagship Broadcasting House headquarters, one of the key questions facing the then head of news, Richard Sambrook, was where to place News Online. For Sambrook, the dilemma was "all that was special in the way News Online work might simply evaporate when it was brought in closer contact with the rest of the organization" (Küng-Shankleman, 2003: pp. 2–3). When the BBC integrated its news operations at New Broadcasting House in 2013, online journalists were placed at the heart of the news hub in the middle of the building, overlooked by an eight-storey high atrium, with the hope that its "organizational learning" would permeate the rest of the newsroom (Küng-Shankleman, 2003: p. 12).

The question of physical separation or integration of different news actors is fundamental to the ways of working and thinking of the newsroom. Location can serve as a proxy to subordinate challengers or as a means to infuse reinvention. For example, the *New York Times* online newsroom was housed in a separate building to the print operations, until then-executive editor Bill Keller announced in 2005 his intention to bring them together. His memo said the move was intended

> to reorganize our structures and our minds to make Web journalism, in forms that are familiar and yet-to-be-invented, as natural to us as writing and editing, to do all this without losing the essential qualities that makes us *The Times*.
>
> (cited in Strupp, 2006: p. 46)

Mirroring the initial physical separation, BBC News Online started life as an autonomous unit with the overall BBC News structure, with its own newsroom, technical and administrative staff, as well as its own robust budget. It was able to decide on its priorities and allocate resources as it saw fit. At the time, we felt we were operating as an autonomous republic within the larger federation of the BBC. Becoming more integrated incurred the risk that the larger and stronger broadcast side of news would seek "to reinforce the dominant logic, and safeguard the interests of the incumbents" (Fligstein & McAdam, 2011). Institutional backing was key. In the 1990s, the then BBC Director-General John Birt had a strong personal belief in the importance of the Internet and its potential to extend the BBC's mission to explain (Barrett, 2013). The head of BBC News Online, Bob Eggington, made Birt's vision possible. Eggington was "a strong leader with maverick tendencies" (Küng-Shankleman, 2003). As one staff member recalled, "Bob put up a wall around the team stopping harmful external interference" (quoted in Orlowski, 2012).

Eggington took to heart his role of defending the unit from interference from the rest of the BBC and fostered a culture of urgency, creativity and problem-solving. The sense of haste and speed felt by the team has similarities with the culture fostered by Silicon Valley giants in the 2000s to "move fast and break things" (for an overview, see Taplin, 2017). When Eggington was first told it would take two years and 12 programmers to create the technical infrastructure for the site, he insisted it could be done in 16 weeks with five programmers (Orlowski, 2012). Speed was central as Eggington feared that the longer it took to launch, the higher the risk of interference from established parts of the BBC. By comparison, years later the development and launch of the corporation's on-demand service, the iPlayer, was mired in delay, reflecting the number of BBC units involved in the process (Orlowski, 2012).

Moving fast, without following all the minutiae of BBC protocols and procedures, was radical within the corporation and contributed to the feeling of a start-up that was challenging existing ways of doing things. For example, a staff member said that setting up a new sub-section in the site's navigation involved walking over to the editor-in-chief, Mike Smartt, getting a verbal approval and "half an hour later we had it on the site" (Küng-Shankleman, 2003: p. 9). This is certainly how I recall those times. As daily news editor from 1997 to 2001, I had significant autonomy from counterparts in radio and TV to decide on editorial priorities and resource allocation. The set-up of the unit meant we functioned as institutional entrepreneurs, working in an unstable field but with the vision, freedom and resources to create and execute on a "common project" (Lawrence & Suddaby, 2006: p. 249).

In her analysis of the creation and development of BBC News Online, Küng-Shankleman notes that it "was right from the start a focused entity, and thanks to its independent status, able to concentrate on its news service and avoid the fabled BBC bureaucracy" (2003: p. 8). The set-up of BBC News Online, both physically and organizationally, highlights key factors identified by Küng-Shankleman in her work on innovation in digital news. It points to the importance of what she says is the "blending of journalistic, technological and commercial competencies involving a deep integration of tech into editorial processes, the presence of digital editorial thinkers and content creation processes that are content and data driven" (Küng-Shankleman, 2015, xi).

Processes

This physical separation contributed to the development of an intellectual separation concerning how the online team conceived of its journalism. The creation of BBC News Online allowed for the introduction of novel practices in news production at the BBC, albeit within the overarching public service imperative of the organization. With its own staff and resourcing, and a high level of independence, the set-up of BBC News Online created opportunities for experimenting with novel forms of storytelling and exploring emerging online tools. The team pioneered online practices that have become identified with the professional identity of the digital journalist – such as speed and immediacy, iterative updates, multimedia storytelling, the integration of user-generated content and audience analytics. These are captured in the unit's internal guidebook (BBC News Interactive, 2005), which served as a playbook for the journalists. It included guidelines for sourcing, accuracy and impartiality, as well as stressing the importance of speed, brevity in writing, headlines and links (BBC News Interactive, 2005). I used to only half-jokingly tell my team, the deadline is always now (Robins, 1999).

However, journalistic rules and routines were firmly based in core BBC values of accuracy, impartiality, independence and accountability. What BBC News Online did is rearticulate what these ideals meant given the conceptual changes inherent in a digital and networked environment. New technologically specific forms were deployed as opportunities to reinvent what BBC journalism could be in a digital age. BBC News Online's editor, Pete Clifton, said that "our success has been driven by journalistic excellence, boundless energy and a willingness to take chances, innovate and learn some lessons along the way" (quoted in BBC News Interactive Guidebook, 2005: p. 3).

One example of the readiness to experiment was evident in the approach to data journalism at BBC News Online. The aim of data journalism was threefold, according to Hurrell and Leimdorfer: "enable a reader to discover information that is personally relevant; reveal a story that is remarkable and previously unknown; and help the reader to better understand a complex issue" (2012: p. 29). These aims reflect the BBC's mission to explain and the journalistic newshound approach identified by Borges-Rey in his study of data journalism in the U.K. (2017). But there is also an emphasis on empowering audiences to interact and connect with data. An early example came in 1999, when the site published government data on school league tables in a way that enabled users to find their school and compare it with others. The focus of these projects was to help people find "personally relevant snippets of information. These tools appeal to the time-poor who may not choose to explore lengthy analysis" (Hurrell & Leimdorfer, 2012: p. 29).

Perhaps more significantly, the people involved in data journalism spanned various disciplines. The "Specials" team as it was known, brought together journalists, developers and designers. Housed in a room next to the newsroom, the team was responsible for producing short and longer-term interactive content, infographics and data visualizations for the website, with a high degree of internal autonomy (Dick, 2014). The mix of editorial, code and design foreshadowed the interactive and data teams created in the 2000s at organizations such as the *New York Times*. In Canada, the *Globe and Mail* stands out as having a Visual Journalism team that brings together expertise from a range of domains, including data.

Platforms

Technologically specific forms of journalistic work give rise to discourses of continuity, resistance or renewal (Powers, 2012). In the case of BBC News Online, there was a significant interplay between journalism and technology. The technical backbone of the website was developed by an independent team, even though, in 1996, the BBC had handed over rights to Fujitsu ICL to use BBC material and build its websites, including news, funded by advertising. Director-General John Birt took news out of the deal, as he believed "it was unthinkable you could put that service like that out with advertisements" (quoted in Orlowski, 2012: p. 1). Advertising was anathema to the ethos of the public service broadcaster in the U.K.

The experience of BBC News Online shows how the technology was developed hand-in-hand with editorial priorities in mind, including the Content Production System (CPS) that was built in-house. The aim was to "allow journalists to be journalists, freeing them from the need to grapple with the technology underlying the Internet, and second, that it should ensure absolute reliability for users" (Küng-Shankleman, 2003: p. 12). The section on the CPS in the unit's guidebook stressed that "it is vital that you feel comfortable using the CPS so that you can concentrate on the important element – the journalism" (BBC News Interactive, 2005: p. 21).

The online publishing platform, CPS, was far from perfect and it would crash from time to time. But at the time, it was one of the most advanced content management system for news, intended to be able to "juggle 60 in-house staff hammering it at once, publishing stories, with many more feeds coming in from other places" (Orlowski, 2012: p. 2). The lead developer of CPS, Matthew Karas, deemed existing online publishing systems to be too complex or ill-suited to cope with editorial demands (Orlowski, 2012). As one of the most well-resourced public broadcasters in the world, and with the institutional backing of Director-General John Birt, Karas and his team were able to draw on significant funding and resources to develop an in-house solution to its editorial needs. Back then, there was no off-the-shelf third-party system that could be used by dozens of journalists at the same time, enable them to easily produce multimedia stories and send them live within 30 seconds, without having to worry about HTML. As Orlowski notes "a huge degree of trust was placed on the techies to build the world's most demanding news content management system – which paid off" (2012: p. 4). His account charts how the technical team was driven by a sense of urgency, looking for workarounds and fixes so that the site could go live on schedule in late 1997. In this context, technology was serving as both an exemplar of continuity by bolstering existing BBC News values and as a basis for the reinvention of the journalist with a range of digital production skills. For Powers, "novel technical skills combined with innovative journalistic thinking are viewed as reinvention's basis" (2012: p. 43).

There were also discourses of resistance to technology from some at the BBC that mirrored what was happening in the broader industry in the late 1990s (and to a certain extent still today). Powers (2012) highlights how digital means of production was seen by some as a challenge to the field stability of journalism because it appeared lawless and chaotic while threatening core occupational values. A discussion of the technologies of data journalism surfaces similar tensions as journalists with new digital and data skill sets can be viewed as either agents of continuity and/or disruption.

Book outline

Data journalism serves as a more recent example to examine journalism's DNA strands and their evolutionary development after two decades of digitization and digitalization (Padgett & Powell, 2012). Twenty years on, we examine data journalism as a site to consider how far digitalization, together with novel social and non-human networks, have created pathways for social and material relations that construct legitimate ways for being a journalist and doing journalism. We focus on Canada as the domain for analysis to surface how a subspecialty of journalist is positioning itself in the light of multiple crises in journalism. Canada serves as an example of a mature media system facing decline in for-profit media, with high levels of concentration of ownership, a prominent public service broadcaster and growing government commitments to open data (Legault, 2015; Picard, 2016; Winseck, 2016). Data journalism practices, forms, roles and identities emerge differently depending on the national contexts, with some of the main distinctions not surprisingly involving the relationship between technology and traditional notions of journalistic identity, resourcing and government approaches to open data (Borges-Rey, 2016).

We begin in Chapter 1 by casting a critical perspective on the ubiquity of the concept of disruption in journalism by drawing on literatures from organizational and institutional theory, and innovation theory. We examine the notion of hybridity in the field of journalism, using data journalism to consider questions of organizational orientation, rebranded and emergent professional identities and their contributions to maintaining journalism in the midst of crises, conflict and change. We shift away from binary discourses of the death or reinvention of journalism to find evidence of how data journalism has adapted and is adapting. We find the growth of a subspeciality of journalist (Usher, 2016), newer networks, actors and actants, along with emergent norms, methods and epistemologies such as collaboration and computational thinking. We suggest that data journalists are capable of mobilizing discursive, technological and, in well-resourced newsrooms, financial assets, to advance maintenance and regeneration in journalism.

We build on these ideas in Chapter 2 which considers data journalism as a form of "liquid journalism." This chapter investigates the interrelated challenges of practice and research in a field with blurred and porous boundaries, differing understandings of the domain, overlapping and divergent organizational titles and structures, fluidity of roles and responsibilities, and evolving and shifting tools and technologies. We argue that the messiness of data journalism as a field opens up opportunities for competing epistemologies and expertise, as emerging and established actors interact to (re)assert power and authority.

In Chapter 3, we turn our focus to how the phenomenon of both formal and informal collaboration in data journalism plays out against the long-standing norm in 20th-century journalism of competition. The phenomenon exhibits itself in formal projects that engage actors from different disciplines, as well as in informal exchanges between journalists working for competing news outlets. Collaboration emerges from the interdisciplinary nature of data journalism, limited institutional resources and a shared sense of identity and mission. We find data journalists actively advancing and taking advantage of instability and crises around trust in journalism, newer competitors and a shifting relationship with the audience, furthering their own interests and identity through an emergent community of practice. Collaboration within and outside the profession is mobilized to legitimize new norms, conventions and practices, and advance a journalism that is cast as more open, transparent and accountable.

In Chapter 4, we look at data journalism through the lens of materiality, considering tools and technologies as actants. By examining the materiality of data journalism, we seek to open up the epistemological implications of the "black box" of technologies. The chapter draws on literature from Science and Technology Studies to unpack how technology and journalistic methods are shaped by the nature of the data and tools available, the limitations of news routines, resourcing and the level of expertise in the newsroom. Lifting the lid on the black box of data journalism reveals how free and easy-to-use tools, adopted in less well-resourced newsrooms, can both advance a journalist's competencies and limit their agency and capacity to derive and share meaning from data.

The burgeoning industry of data journalism education is tackled in Chapter 5. The growth in learning opportunities in data journalism are indicative of shifting demand for skills and knowledge, as well as professional development in journalism from students and professionals able and willing to pay for them. We find that data journalism education is largely evolving along traditional ways of journalistic knowing, focused on the ability to produce journalism around recognizable forms and purposes in a specific technical and political economic context. We suggest that the prevalence of this type of data journalism education reflects the persisting habits of using journalism genres to ground journalism education in established and familiar forms. Here we also find evidence of experimentation with a number of schools partnering with computer science colleagues and departments creating courses and programs that try to bridge these domains.

In the concluding chapter we build on the previous chapters by conceptualizing change and its relationship to journalism, using the lens of data journalism. We consider how technological and professional adaption emerges in journalism through a (dis)continuous evolution of norms, practices, relationships and technologies. Innovation is both iterative and sustained, taking place within broader organizational, technological and social contexts, as data journalists seek to exert power and agency given the instability of journalism in the 21st century. The multiple crises in journalism have created apertures in long-standing norms and practices for data journalists to advance alternative and novel ways of doing and knowing. We note instances of innovation and technological adaptation around data journalism where journalists are able to harness investment and resourcing, with examples of blended identities combining journalist, programmer and coder. These blended actors bring with them different ways of doing and knowing, serving as bridges between maintenance and regeneration in the newsroom.

As in the early days of BBC News Online, and in digital journalism in general, data journalism serves as a site to examine change in journalism. Both are associated with technologically specific forms of work that were greeted as an extension of existing practices, as threats to be contained and/or as opportunities for reinvention (Powers, 2012). Much as in this introduction I have tracked the threads of the rise and growth of digital journalism as seen through the prism of my personal experience, in this book we trace the emergence and flourishing of data journalism through a scholarly lens.

References

Barnhurst, K. (1994) *Seeing the Newspaper*. New York, NY: St. Martin's.

Barrett, C. (2013) John Birt back to see what he started. *Ariel*, November 21. Available from: www.bbc.co.uk/ariel/25019286 [Accessed 15 July 2018].

BBC News Interactive. (2005) Guidebook, BBC. 2005 Edition.

BBC News Website. (2004) OBE for BBC website founder. June 12. Available from: http://news.bbc.co.uk/2/hi/uk_news/3799141.stm [Accessed 15 July 2018].

Boczkowski, P. J. (2004) *Digitizing the News: Innovation in Online Newspapers*. Boston, MA: MIT Press.

Borges-Rey, E. (2016) Unravelling data journalism: A study of data journalism practice in British newsrooms. *Journalism Practice*. 10(7), 833–843.

Borges-Rey, E. (2017) Towards an epistemology of data journalism in the devolved nations of the United Kingdom: Changes and continuities in materiality, performativity and reflexivity. *Journalism*. 1–18. DOI: 10.1177/1464884917693864

Brennen, J. S., & Kreiss, D. (2016) Digitalization. In: Jensen, K. B., Rothenbuhler, E. W., Pooley, J. D., & Craig, R. T. (eds.). *The International Encyclopedia of Communication Theory and Philosophy*. Chichester, West Sussex: Wiley-Blackwell, pp. 556–566.

Dick, M. (2014) Interactive infographics and news values. *Digital Journalism*. 2(4), 490–506.

Domingo, D. (2008) Interactivity in the daily routines of online newsrooms: Dealing with an uncomfortable myth. *Journal of Computer-Mediated Communication*. 13(3), 680–704.

Fligstein, N., & McAdam, D. (2011) Toward a general theory of strategic action fields. *Sociological Theory*. 29(1), 1–26.

Gieryn, T. F. (2000) A space for place in sociology. *Annual Review of Sociology*. 26, 463–496.

Hurrell, B., & Leimdorfer, A. (2012) Data journalism at the BBC. In: Gray, J., Chambers, L., & Bounegru, L. (eds.). *The Data Journalism Handbook: How Journalists Can Use Data to Improve the News*. Sebastopol, CA: O'Reilly Media, p. 29.

Küng, L., Leandros, N., Picard, R. G., Schroeder, R., & Van der Wurff, R. (2008) The impact of the Internet on media organisation strategies and structures. In: Küng, L., Picard, R., & Towse, R. (eds.). *The Internet and the Mass Media*. Los Angeles: Sage.

Küng-Shankleman, L. (2003) When old dogs learn new tricks: The launch of BBC News Online. *European Case Clearing House*, 119-1.

Lawrence, T. B., & Suddaby, R. (2006) Institutions and institutional work. In: Clegg, S. R., Hardy, C., Lawrence, T. B., & Nord, W. R. (eds.). *Sage Handbook of Organization Studies*, 2nd Edition. London: Sage, pp. 215–254.

Legault, S. (2015) Striking the right balance for transparency. *Office of the Information Commissioner of Canada*. Available from: www.ci-oic.gc.ca/eng/rapport-%20de%20modernisation-modernization-report.aspx [Accessed 3 September 2018].

Lowrey, W. (2002) Word people vs. picture people: Normative differences and strategies of control over work among newsroom subgroups. *Mass Communication and Society*. 5, 411–432.

Orlowski, A. (2012) Scoop! The inside story of the news website that saved the BBC. *The Register*, November 28. Available from: www.theregister.co.uk/2012/11/28/the_bbc_news_online_story/ [Accessed 15 July 2018].

Padgett, J. F., & Powell, W. W. (2012) *The Emergence of Organizations and Markets*. Princeton, NJ: Princeton University Press.

Picard, R. (2016) Submission to the House of Commons Standing Committee on Canadian Heritage, Local Media Inquiry, Email Sent to Mary Lynn Young, October 1.

Powers, M. (2012) In forms that are familiar and yet-to-be invented: American journalism and the discourse of technologically specific work. *Journal of Communication*. 36(1), 24–43.

Robins, J. (1999) The global correspondent: BBC News Online helps people in a disaster to trace their relatives and file their own stories: Is this the future? *The Independent*, August 24.

Singer, J. B., Domingo, D., Heinonen, A., Hermida, A., Paulussen, S., Quandt, T., & Vujnovic, M. (2011) *Participatory Journalism: Guarding Open Gates at Online Newspapers*. Malden, MA: John Wiley & Sons.

Singer, J. B., Tharp, M., & Haruta, A. (1999) Online staffers: Superstars or second-class citizens? *Newspaper Research Journal*. 20, 29–47.

Strupp, J. (2006) The headaches behind the headlines. *Editor & Publisher*, April 30, 139, 40–47.

Taplin, J. (2017) *Move Fast and Break Things: How Facebook, Google, and Amazon Cornered Culture and Undermined Democracy*. New York: Little, Brown, and Company.

Usher, N. (2015) Newsroom moves and the newspaper crisis evaluated: Space, place, and cultural meaning. *Media, Culture & Society*. 37(7), 1005–1021.

Usher, N. (2016) *Interactive Journalism: Hackers, Data, and Code*. Urbana, IL: University of Illinois Press.

Webber, E. (2017) Election 97: The first online election. *BBC News Website*, September 4. Available from: www.bbc.com/news/uk-politics-parliaments-41111242 [Accessed 15 July 2018].

Winseck, D. (2016) Media and Internet concentration in Canada report 1984–2015. *Canadian Media Concentration Research Project*. Available from: www.cmcrp.org/media-and-internet-concentration-in-canada-report-1984-2015/

Zelizer, B. (1995) Journalism's 'last' stand: Wirephoto and the discourse of resistance. *Journal of Communication*. 45, 78–92.

1 Hybrid times*

In 2017, the International Journalism Festival in Perugia, arguably one of the most sought after invitations and well-attended journalism conferences globally, started a crowdsourced document with a call to action. The document was called the "#PerugiaPledge: Creating a set of guidelines for data journalists." It started with: "I will take data as serious as words" (Deutsche Welle Innovation Blog, 2017). The simple phrase encapsulates the ethos of data journalism as a form, process and subspecialty of journalism (Coddington, 2015, 2019; Usher, 2016). Taking a cue from Peters and Broersma (2014), this chapter interrogates why data journalism is having a social, cultural, technological, political and economic moment in journalism. For Peters and Broersma, "by relying on new approaches, technologies and contexts to retell old stories, this is what allows new forms of journalistic storytelling to take hold; to appear, Janus-faced, new and familiar; simultaneously forward-looking while staying true to tradition" (2014: p. xii).

Data journalism is indeed Janus-faced in that it looks backwards and forwards at the same time. There are any number of rationales for the growing global embrace of data journalism, elements of which some suggest have been prevalent for hundreds of years, basically as long as news stories have used data. Others link it to the advent of computer-assisted reporting, which first got its start in the United States when CBS used one of the early computers – the UNIVAC – to predict the election outcome in 1952 between Dwight D. Eisenhower and Adlai Stevenson (Howard, 2014). Although the computer's first foray into news appeared to be less than a good fit and the machine itself "received very little airtime" (Bochannek, 2012: para. 11). Bochannek claimed that,

> After Charles Collingwood introduced the "fabulous electronic machine," he struggled to describe its operation and components. Items new to the viewer were presented in familiar and unthreatening terms:

> See those round things over there, looks kind of like candy mints? Well, those are reels of metallic tape.
>
> (Bochannek, 2012: para. 11)

Finally, according to Bochannek, “when it was time for UNIVAC to shine, Collingwood anthropomorphized the machine: ‘Have you got a prediction for us, UNIVAC?’ UNIVAC did not answer” (Bochannek, 2012: para. 11).

What UNIVAC did have is the answer to the election, correctly predicting that Eisenhower would win in 1952. However, its early results were held back for fear of getting it wrong:

> It isn’t clear if Remington Rand or CBS held back the predictions, but Remington Rand representative Art Draper came on the air after midnight: “As more votes came in, the odds came back and it was obviously evident that we should have had the nerve enough to believe the machine in the first place. It was right. We were wrong. Next year we’ll believe it.”
>
> (Bochannek, 2012: para. 14)

Decades later, a distrust of data in elections seems to linger. Following the rise and eventual electoral presidential victory of Donald Trump in 2016, U.S. newspaper headlines lamented the failure of data-driven predictions. Some questioned whether “the data renaissance emerged at the wrong time” (Taylor, 2016: para. 4) or called for a return to “old-school reporting tactics” (Guess, 2016: p. 2). Setting aside the problem of conflating data journalism with electoral outcomes, the example underscores tensions at the core of this book: how the domain of data journalism serves as a meaningful site to examine organizational change, expertise, technology and power.

Why data journalism?

We began studying data journalism in 2013 when we received our first grant to examine an early example of algorithmic news, the Homicide Report, at the *Los Angeles Times* through interviews with journalists. This was a year after the first awards category recognizing data journalism was launched in 2012 signaling an industry-wide recognition of the genre as believable and here to stay (Young, Hermida & Fulda, 2018). As journalism scholars and former journalists with expertise in digital media, sociology of news and crime newsmaking, we were initially interested in how this genre and subspecialty of non-human journalism was adding to what we know about the nature of crime news, and technological change more generally in journalism organizations (Usher, 2016). Our results showed an uneven adaptation and interrelationship between shifting definitions of crime news, professional expertise, technologies and practices rooted in history and newsroom economics, with the programmer and algorithm assuming a role in who gets to define homicide news.

Since that time we have extended our study of data journalism. For this book, we draw from our five years of research on data journalism and its wider field of practice in regional and national newsrooms and beyond in two countries including 25 interviews, site visits and a content analysis of data journalism awards submissions (Hermida & Young, 2017; Young & Hermida, 2015; Young, Hermida & Fulda, 2018). We chose this site of journalism practice because of its clear linkages to the past and future to understand how it is articulating and unfolding in the present. Methodologically, we have focused in part on journalists and journalism organizations that situate themselves in the middle so as not to skew the results towards the small percentage of journalistic outliers who work at well-funded internationally recognized organizations (Appelgren & Nygren, 2014; Stencel, Adair & Kamalakanthan, 2014).

We have been specifically interested in Canada, a country with a journalism ecosystem that includes a public broadcaster, largely small to mid-size journalism organizations, a commitment to open data and high level of concentration of media ownership across journalism industries particularly with respect to vertical integration (Picard, 2016). According to Robert Picard in a 2016 submission to a federal inquiry on the state of local news, local news firms "central to news provision" operate as "near monopolies." Picard further describes elements of the journalism landscape as, "national broadcasters and papers provide national and international news, but sources are quite limited for provincial and local news in most of Canada's municipalities and communities" (2016: np).[1] In addition, there have been significant job losses across the journalism sector in Canada. Skelton (2018) identified a 7 per cent decline in the absolute number of journalists in the country over the 21st century, from 12,965 in 2001 to 12,050 in 2016. This equates to a 20 per cent decrease in journalists' relative share of the labor market over this period (Skelton, 2018). For their part, Lindgren and Corbett (2018) noted the closure of 248 local news outlets across Canada from 2008 to 2018. Against this background, a recent report on the state of the industry for the federal government advocated for financial support of the journalism industry, with one recommendation specifically supporting "the use of data and evidence in journalism" as it is linked to excellence in civic journalism (Public Policy Forum, 2017: p. 88).

By locating our research in one country, we propose to decenter the concept of disruption by extending our approach to change beyond the economic and single news organization or industry level. We focus on one subspecialty of journalistic actors – the data journalist – across institutional contexts. Our approach considers data journalists and their non-human actors, as at the coalface of a number of crises in the field of journalism, which includes new competitors, such as big technology platforms, and participatory publics (Bell, Owen, Brown, Hauka & Rashidian, 2017; Callison & Young, forthcoming; Fligstein & McAdam, 2011; Freelon, McIlwain & Clark, 2018; Singer et al., 2011). We find after almost 20 years and the phases of Web 1.0 and Web 2.0,[2] that the incursion of data journalism and journalists, novel social and non-human networks, are setting the stage for a growing subspecialty of journalism in Canada (Usher, 2016). We argue that this subspecialty is able to operate as strategic actors and "institutional entrepreneurs" who are collectively gaining advantage as a result of these crises that have foregrounded questions of legitimacy of journalism[3] (Anderson, 2018; Boczkowski & Papacharissi, 2018; Broersma, 2010b; Callison & Young, forthcoming; DiMaggio, 1988; Fligstein & McAdam, 2011; Lawrence & Suddaby, 2006). We draw in part from institutional and organizational theory and suggest that data journalists are able to access important discursive, technological and in well-funded institutions, financial resources, supporting a process of rebranding and emergent expertise that prioritizes maintenance of journalism authority and regeneration of the field of journalism (Anderson, 2018; Fligstein & McAdam, 2011; Lawrence & Suddaby, 2006; Lowrey, 2012).

Here we find emergent relations with both human and non-human actors, from inside and outside of legacy journalism fields of influence, are creating the context for newer expertise, networks and power relations. These are supporting newer forms, such as a range of data visualization expertise, and epistemologies including norms and mindsets such as collaboration and computational thinking as well as players from academics to non-human actors, platforms and audiences that however still largely align with traditional news ideologies (Borges-Rey, 2017; Küng, 2015). Lowrey's (2012) research on the emergence of health news blogs and how online news sites developed in two urban contexts in two separate case studies in the U.S. is relevant to the development of data journalism forms that we address in the book. His findings largely reflect his institutional model, which predicted that "over time innovative news forms and practices emerge in variation, flock together in a selection process, stabilize, and then demonstrate retention. Forms and practices survive [are selected] initially when they settle within niches" (2012: p. 216). He goes on to suggest that "over time, surviving variations gain stability. . . . When the forms and practices become accepted, they are considered institutionalized and secured by their shared understandings and dependencies" (Lowrey, 2012: p. 216.). In Chapter 4, we find a settling of forms taking place with respect to maps and graphing applications that are shaping the nature of data journalism, both empowering journalists and adding to their precarity, while creating institutional dependency on certain platforms.

These shifts however have to be situated alongside much of the literature on the impact of digitalization and change in the sociology of journalism organizations over this period. This research has found a stubborn persistence of pre-Internet norms, practices, identities, structures and orientations, with a keen eye towards technological disruption and its possibilities for the future (Boczkowski, 2004; Domingo, 2008; Singer et al., 2011). These approaches indicate a necessary preoccupation with understanding past structures and ways of being a journalist, along with ideals of innovation as ways to adapt to the impact digitalization. That this moment is increasingly complicated and still "liquid" is not in question. Journalists continue to have to navigate rationalization, deinstitutionalization, casualization, automation, technological change and the conflicts and cultural shifts embedded in these processes following the relative homogeneity of journalism that preceded this era (Picard, 2014). The next section of this chapter examines how disruptive innovation has been discussed within journalism, separate from the wider literature on the impacts of digitalization and technological, ending with a discussion of data journalism specifically.

Disrupting disruption

We have been drawn to data journalism for the past five years because it is at the coalface at a number of key journalism concerns, and we see it as a site of regeneration and settling in the field, following from the many accounts that have examined and articulated the impacts of disruption on journalism more generally. In an incisive and well-executed example, Clayton Christensen teamed up with David Skok and James Allworth to write about disruptive innovation's impact on journalism in *Nieman Reports* in 2012 http://niemanreports.org/articles/breaking-news/. The article, provocatively titled "Breaking News," was written as a prescriptive to the journalism industry to facilitate its survival after the 2008 financial crisis while "mired in the innovator's dilemma: A false choice between today's revenues and tomorrow's digital promise" (2012: p. 6). They identify cautionary tales in classic journalism disruptors such as *Time* Magazine (now legacy media), which launched in the early 20th century and built its model of "rewrites" as a "rip-and-read copy from the day's major publications" (2012: p. 6) to 21st-century digital-only outlets such as the *Huffington Post* and *Buzzfeed*. They indicate the latter two organizations began their move up the value chain as "news aggregators" eventually becoming "generators of original content" (2012: p. 6).

Christensen, Skok and Allworth go on to prescribe three post disruption options for journalism's future: (1) create a framework "for what it is audiences value;" (2) assess the "impact of disruption on traditional newsroom business models . . . and ways to exploit other aspects of the value network;" and (3) examine "the role of cultures and capabilities in an organization and how best to manage them" (2012: p. 8). They end with an assessment of the cause of past failures and some advice: "The reason that innovation often seems to be so difficult for established newsrooms is that, though they employ highly capable people, they are working within organizational structures whose processes and priorities weren't designed for the task at hand" (2012: p. 20). Necessary change for them involves creating an "innovative newsroom environment," which they identify as "looking within the existing value network and beyond traditional business models to discover new experiences for audiences, then realigning your resources, processes and priorities to embrace these disruptions" (2012: p. 20).

What the article didn't do is question the wide use of disruptive innovation and how its discursive promiscuity might be having an impact on how we talk about and think about change at this time, and what we could and should do for journalism. A 20-year retrospective on the impact of the theory of disruptive innovation following pointed critique by Harvard University historian Jill Lepore in the *New Yorker* on the theory's generic and wide deployment takes on the term's wide terrain. Christensen, Raynor and McDonald (2015) acknowledge the "broad usage" of a term originally intended as a specific economic experience to describe the advent and impact of a lower cost, often smaller competitor, on a market and incumbent(s).[4] Lepore goes on to claim that since Christensen first wrote *The Innovator's Dilemma*, "everyone is either disrupting or being disrupted" (Lepore, 2014: p. 30). In their retrospective, Christensen et al. lament for the most part that "the theory's core concepts have been widely misunderstood and its basic tenets frequently misapplied" (2015: p. 46). They go on to critique how the theory has been used "loosely to invoke the concept of innovation . . . to describe *any* situation in which an industry is shaken up and previously successful incumbents stumble" (2015: p. 46 *italics* in original).

In addition to the over- and mis-usage of the term, Lepore critiques Christensen's original method in identifying the disruptive innovation model, and argues for a more historically attuned reading of some of the concepts that are relevant to journalism. First, she argues that disruptive innovation is a predictive model that does not live up to its promise because it is based on selective case studies. Here she identifies concerns about how the model is now applied to sectors that prioritize values and obligations other than profit and economics, such as universities, health care and journalism. For Lepore, disruptive innovation has become "a theory of history founded on a profound anxiety about financial collapse, an apocalyptic fear of global devastation, and shaky evidence" (2014: p. 31). She cites an example from journalism as evidence: "Last month, days after the *Times*' publisher, Arthur Sulzberger, Jr., fired Jill Abramson, the paper's executive editor, the *Times*' 2014 Innovation Report was leaked. It includes graphs inspired by Christensen's *The Innovator's Dilemma*, along with a lengthy, glowing summary of the book's key arguments" (Lepore, 2014: p. 31). Lepore goes on to quote from the report:

> Disruption is a predictable pattern across many industries in which fledgling companies use new technology to offer cheaper and inferior alternatives to products sold by established players [think Toyota taking on Detroit decades ago]. Today, a pack of news startups are hoping to "disrupt" our industry by attacking the strongest incumbent – *The New York Times*.
>
> (2014: p. 31)

She goes on to describe the disruptors: "they seem so tiny and powerless, until you realize, but only after it's too late, that they're devastatingly dangerous. . . . Think of it this way: The *Times* is a nation-state: *BuzzFeed* is stateless. Disruptive innovation is competitive strategy for an age seized by terror" (2014: p. 31). Lepore's other main critique is that the model is ahistorical, and does not address how change happens, or consider the social construction of concepts such as innovation relative to their historical contexts. For example, she locates the term innovation historically as "the idea of progress stripped of the aspirations of the Enlightenment, scrubbed clean of the horrors of the twentieth century" (2014: p. 32). Her conclusion is that the theory of disruptive innovation is best understood as about "why businesses fail," not why change happens or the ability to prognosticate on who or what is going to succeed and fail.

As the title of this book series suggests, disruption has infiltrated journalism. And as Lepore argues with respect to understanding disruptive innovation historically, systems, individuals and organizational change are more complicated than an atavistic binary choice between adapt or be left behind, particularly in sectors such as journalism that make claims to public service. Has the general use of disruption in journalism distracted from critical perspectives about the relationships and causes of disruption and stability in journalism and how they have shifted over time? These include understanding change in journalism from sociological and organizational approaches, as well as ones that link change to larger social, cultural, political, economic, market, technological and structural forces (Borges-Rey, 2017; Callison & Young, forthcoming; Küng, 2015). For example, Anderson's book on data journalism is an excellent example of research that approaches change over time historically, telling a compelling story of continuity about journalists' increasing attempts "to render their knowledge claims more certain, contextual and explanatory" (2018: p. 1) since the middle of the 20th century.[5] Our addition is to assess and understand change within a subspecialty of journalism in a specific national context. In the next section, we briefly explore technological change and hybridity in journalism.

Technological change and hybridity in journalism

A common but not absolute framing in some of the organizational journalism literature on data journalism appears to be an either/or relationship to the role and impact of technology, the past/historical understanding of norms and practice, and future success. Boczkowski's (2004) study of online newsrooms found that the ability of print newsrooms to take advantage of the web and innovate was affected by three main characteristics. These included:

> Relationships between the print or online newsrooms as either close or distant, the representation of the intended user as either consumer or producer of information and either technically savvy or unsavvy, and the character of online newsroom practices as either reproducing editorial gatekeeping or generating alternatives to it.
>
> (Boczkowski, 2004: pp. 171–172)

Chadwick (2013) addresses the tendency of either/or thinking in past analyses of media and advocates for a shift in approach that takes systems thinking into account. For him, the Internet is an open system (as opposed to a closed system of self orientation and reproduction), encouraging perspectives that consider the "evolving interrelationships among older and newer media logics" (Chadwick, 2013: p. ix) and hybridity. While we situate ourselves in established sociological approaches to newsroom organization (Schudson, 1989) that identify the importance of examining and understanding intra-organizational norms and practice, we also look to the larger context of systems thinking and scholarship on media hybridity in order to account for evolving individual and collective agency and "social differentiation" that involve technology and power within and across media (Chadwick, 2013: p. 18). A number of scholars have already staked out their territory in this space, including researchers who have identified the tensions and continuities in this emergent hybrid media context of data/computational journalists.

Ananny and Crawford (2015) suggest that the shift to a greater incorporation of data in news is inevitable; it is just how that transition is going to occur. Through evidence from interviews with mobile news application designers in Europe, the United States and the United Kingdom, they point to the creation of an "emerging liminal press: a set of field level relationships among actors who may not self-identify as journalists but nonetheless define the conditions under which news is created and circulates" (Ananny & Crawford, 2015: p. 193). These new actors are shaped by their networks and generate new journalism practices "that span multiple professional identities, information ideologies and assumptions about how news and public life intersect" (Ananny & Crawford, 2015: pp. 192–193).

While acknowledging some of the critiques of Chadwick's system of hybridity and power (Witschge, Anderson, Domingo & Hermida, 2018), it is useful in understanding this landscape. It provides a more complex framework and understanding of technological change in media that supports a nuanced ability to interrogate past assumptions around journalistic agency and power as well as its relationship to expertise and the public. Questions of power in this approach emerge from the context of shared economic, cultural, organizational norms and practices with the new and old in constant relationship such that "embedding norms and acting with regularity are important parts of exercising power in any system" (Chadwick, 2013: p. 18).

"Explosion" of data journalism literature

Data journalism is gaining growing attention from researchers with talk of "an explosion in data journalism-oriented scholarship" (Fink & Anderson, 2015: p. 476). An overview of the literature published in 2017 identified 40 scholarly works published between 1996 and 2015, concluding "there has been an increase of research publications on data journalism and related fields since 2010" (Ausserhofer, Gutounig, Oppermann, Matiasek & Goldgruber, 2017: p. 9). As a side note, the research team only considered works in English and German, and excluded items such as press reports, blog posts and popular textbooks "due to the high number of publications" (2017: p. 2). Indeed, to give an indication of the blossoming field of data journalism, a search for the term on Google Scholar in mid-2018 brought up 4,250 results.

An initial wave of research sought to capture the rise of data journalism in newsrooms concurrent with the digitalization of information and emergence of the Internet. Much of the work examined the phenomenon of data journalism to illuminate how far it could be considered a novel form of journalism that stood apart from other forms such as investigative journalism or computer-assisted reporting (for example, Royal & Blasingame, 2015). One of the preoccupations in the research is whether there are key characteristics that define data journalism as a product (see Chapter 2 for a full discussion).

These elements included the types of visualizations used and the levels of user interaction (Appelgren, 2017, 2018; Knight, 2015; Young, Hermida & Fulda, 2018). Another element is an ethos of openness and transparency, either by involving citizens in gathering or analysing data or by making the raw data publicly available (Borges-Rey, 2016, 2019; Boyles & Meyer, 2016; Karlsen & Stavelin, 2014).

By far, the greatest amount of attention has been on data journalism as a process, with scholars seeking to detail the routines, roles and responsibilities of the actors involved in its production. The most common method has been qualitative interviews to chart the epistemologies of data journalists in the context of newsroom structures and organizational culture[6] (Ausserhofer et al., 2017). The range of research offers insights in the political economy of data journalism. The leaders in this field tend to be large, well-resourced news organizations that have made an institutional investment in this area by creating dedicated data journalism teams. The names are a roll call of international media players. They include the *Guardian*, *Financial Times* (Borges-Rey, 2016) and the BBC (Dick, 2014) in the U.K., and the *New York Times* in the U.S. (Fink & Anderson, 2015; Royal, 2012). The picture in Canada is no different, with only two national news outlets devoting significant resources to the domain (Hermida & Young, 2017). The stratification is evidence of what we have called a "hierarchy of hybridity," with degrees of technological and journalistic blending and amplification of power across journalists and news organizations. In circumstances where there has been an investment in interactive or data teams, there are signs of growing power and the ability to mobilize technological adaptation, journalism and audience imperatives in generative ways. In Canadian research, we found that two national organizations in particular – the public broadcaster and a legacy newspaper – showed significant evidence of agency and capacity with regards to data journalism.

We also noted the emergence of blended techno cultures within data journalism, together with blended identities of data journalists. This illustrates how data journalism as an emergent and fluid field has, in some circumstances, created opportunities for "the successful creation of reserved domains of power" (Chadwick, 2013: p. 44). Various studies have surfaced the rise of the programmer-journalist as a professional category spanning two distinct domains of technology and journalistic identity (Lewis & Usher, 2013; Lewis & Zamith, 2017). The intermingled identity was noted in a study of computer-assisted reporting and data journalism in Chicago (Parasie & Dagiral, 2013), in our study of the *Los Angeles Times* data team (Young & Hermida, 2015) and in our study of data journalism in Canada (Hermida & Young, 2017).

However, in other contexts, the roles of journalist and programmer are operationalized as distinct and separate identities. Royal's (2012) ethnographic study of the *New York Times'* interactive team found that subjects saw themselves as journalists first, though hacker culture affected journalism production. A similar picture emerges from the U.K. where Hannaford's study of the BBC and the Financial Times identified teams in which "journalists, programmers and developers work closely together to produce multimedia, interactive news products," and that hybrid journo-programmers "do not currently exist in the UK" (2015: p. 14). The research shows the degree of plasticity of professional labeling as journalists span reporting and storytelling on the one side, and programming and coding on the other (Usher, 2016).

The performativity of data journalism

Professional labeling is perhaps one of the most visible signs of the distinctions and conflicts involving the relationship between technology and traditional notions of journalistic identity and epistemologies. At play is a spectrum of identities and epistemologies. Usher has focused on identity, pinpointing data journalists as part of a new subspecialty of interactive journalists (2016), while Borges-Rey has described data journalism as a range of characteristics along a continuum that runs from newshound to techie (2017). He sees the initial approach as the more "traditional journalistic ways of handling and engaging with data," while the second "designates an emergent journalistic approach to data based on more computational logics and mindsets" (2017: p. 2). In the newshound camp, data journalism performativity is employed to uphold and reinforce professional norms and discourses about the role of journalism in terms of its watchdog role as a fourth estate. As a performative discourse, this approach to data journalism serves to signal to audiences the truthfulness and veracity of reporting (Broersma, 2010a).

The newshound framework relates to traditional, investigative and watchdog functions of journalism, drawing on the approaches of precision journalism and computer-assisted reporting (Gynnild, 2014). In-depth, investigative data-driven projects are one of the three forms of data journalism identified by Borges-Rey (2016), with daily turnarounds and lighter, entertaining forms as the other two. Similarly, a 2017 report funded by Google categorized investigative data projects as one of three types of data journalism, noting that "in these news stories, the journalist exposes information or surfaces a story hidden in the data" (Rogers, Schwabish & Bowers, 2017, p. 6). Studies of both data journalists and data journalism projects have pointed to the strong links between data journalism and investigative reporting (Loosen, Reimer & De Silva-Schmidt, 2017; Parasie, 2015; Parasie & Dagiral, 2013; Royal & Blasingame, 2015). Many of the 26 data journalists from the 17 countries (in Africa, Australasia, the Americas and Europe) surveyed by Felle saw "digital data reporting as a key component in the journalists' 'toolkit,'" locating "data within the domain of investigative journalism and as an important device to investigate and tell stories of public interest in an engaging way" (2016: p. 86). A strong investigative data project that went on to change policy and win awards, such as the *Globe and Mail's* Unfounded (see Chapter 3), was held up as a pinnacle of journalism excellence by all of our 2018 interviewees. The presumed linkage between investigative reporting and data journalism has "led to something of a perception that data journalism is all about massive data sets, acquired through acts of journalistic bravery and derring-do" (Knight, 2015: p. 64).

The lens of professional awards further highlights the newshound approach in data journalism, acknowledging that this excludes forms of everyday data journalism (Stalph, 2018). In our study of Canadian award winners and finalists, just over half (14 out of 26) were works of investigative journalism (Young, Hermida & Fulda, 2018). Similarly, an analysis of 225 finalists in what the profession considers as the gold standard in data journalism, the Data Journalism Awards, suggested "that awarded projects are slightly more sophisticated and oriented towards fulfilling journalism's watchdog role through investigation and scrutinising those in power" (Loosen, Reimer & De Silva-Schmidt, 2017: p. 15).

While the newshound approach is more aligned with muckraking tradition of journalism, the techie approach is more firmly aligned with computing logics (Borges-Rey, 2017). This end of the spectrum encompasses collaborations between journalists, programmer-journalists and civil actors as identified by Parasie and Dagiral (2013) in their study of data journalism in Chicago. Borges-Rey also includes Gynnild's (2014) framing of journalism as programming as exemplifying an entrepreneurial approach and computational thinking. The techie approach to data opens the way for new forms and genres rooted in a different epistemological proposition from journalistic conventions. A more computational mindset changes "the fundamental thought system in journalism from descriptive storytelling to abstract reasoning, autonomous research and visualisation of quantitative facts" (Gynnild, 2014: p. 725). Journalists at the techie end of the spectrum are newer actors who are "boundary spanners" (Patru, Lauche, van Kranenburg & Ziggers, 2015: p. 1). They represent the blending of the journalist-technologist role and inject a technoculture into the newsroom. As one of our interviewees at the public broadcaster said, "we're fundamentally changing newsrooms and the way we operate, and the kind of conversations and dialogue that we have with each other" (Interview 6, March 26, 2015).

These blended technologists have significant authority to speak, operating as a "bridge" to create "deep connection" and interrelationships among the technologists and legacy journalists in the newsroom, although not without struggle and "confusion" (Interview 17, December 17, 2015). They align with Gynnild's suggestion of journalism as programming as "an entrepreneurial start-up activity that has evoked considerable interest and sparked the interest for digital innovations in journalism" (2014: p. 721). Journalists taking on blended roles within news organizations are acting as institutional entrepreneurs, negotiating the interplay between journalistic conventions and emergent computational logics.

The notion of "institutional entrepreneurs" comes from DiMaggio who suggested that "new institutions arise when organized actors with sufficient resources (*institutional entrepreneurs*) see in them an opportunity to realize interests that they value highly" (1988: p. 14, *italics* in original). Building on the concept, Fligstein and McAdam argue that "skilled actors" in strategic action fields can "help create and maintain collective identities" particularly in "unstable" fields (2011: p. 7). Data journalism emerges as one such field, characterized by blurred and porous boundaries, with hybrid roles, forms and practices.

Conclusion

Our vantage point in this book allows us to chart the impact of iterative innovation, the regenerative potential of "branchings" and "recombinations" within journalism (Padgett & Powell, 2012: p. 2) and some settling in the field. Data journalism offers such a site to assess journalism almost 20 years after the impact of digitalization, and the decade or more since some of the first disruptive innovations in journalism such as YouTube, Facebook, Twitter and *Buzzfeed.* The notion that an emerging settling exists provides the opportunity for an important narrative correction. It allows us to shift from the fear based, victim, survivor binary that can pervade accounts of journalism's recent past that set legacy media victims of disruption versus digital journalism survivors. Instead we can try to clarify the use of disruption by locating disruptive innovation in its appropriate economic context, and in the process unpack stereotypes of technology as binary options of hero or harbinger, and news organizations as disrupting or disrupted. In this sense, we find that this specific domain of journalism has adapted and is adapting, with conflict a generative constant, not a death knell.

Notes

* Contains excerpts from Hermida, A., & Young, M. L. (2017) Finding the data unicorn: A hierarchy of hybridity in data and computational journalism. *Digital Journalism*. 5(2), 159–176.

1 Winseck (2016) convincingly argues that Canadian media ownership has historically shifted, and continues to oscillate between the polarities of concentration and competition. A current additional factor relevant to assessing concentration of journalism in Canada is the public's ability to access a broad range of Internet journalism content (Winseck, 2016).
2 According to Hermida (2015), Web 2.0 "refers to a set of technical changes that allow technically unskilled actors to have dynamic interactions on the Web, facilitating a broad range of activities in the creation, dissemination, and sharing of digital content."
3 See Lawrence and Suddaby (2006) on the increasing "prominence" of institutional research on the "role of actors in the transformation of existing institutions and fields" as well as their discussion of "institutional entrepreneurship" which they identify as "the manner in which interested actors work to influence their institutional contexts through such strategies as technical and market leadership, lobbying for regulatory change and discursive action" (p. 215).
4 According to Christensen, Raynor and McDonald (2015), "'disruption' describes a process whereby a smaller company with fewer resources is able to successfully challenge established incumbent businesses. Specifically, as incumbents focus on improving their products and services for their most demanding [and usually most profitable] customers, they exceed the needs of some segments and ignore the needs of others. Entrants that prove disruptive begin by successfully targeting those overlooked segments, gaining a foothold by delivering more-suitable functionality – frequently at a lower price. Incumbents, chasing higher profitability in more-demanding segments, tend not to respond vigorously. Entrants then move upmarket, delivering the performance that incumbents' mainstream customers require, while preserving the advantages that drove their early success. When mainstream customers start adopting the entrants' offerings in volume, disruption has occurred" (p. 43).
5 In his early research on the risk society, Richard Ericson (1998) argues that data and the sciences are important knowledges to manage risk as they "provide the basis of legal regulation" that "allow institutions to govern at a distance and to include or exclude people as they see fit" (pp. 92–93). He suggests that in this socio-political context, older news genres rooted in the humanities inevitably fall down when held up to the hard facts of and increasing prominence of normal science (see also Hacking, 1990).
6 For example, scholarly studies have looked at data journalists in the United States (Boyles & Meyer, 2016; Fink & Anderson, 2015; Parasie, 2015; Parasie & Dagiral, 2013), the United Kingdom (Borges-Rey, 2016, 2017; Hannaford, 2015), Belgium (De Maeyer Libert, Domingo, Heinderyckx & Le Cam, 2015), Canada (Hermida & Young, 2017; Tabary, Provost & Trottier, 2016), Germany (Weinacht & Spiller, 2014), Norway (Karlsen & Stavelin, 2014) and Sweden (Appelgren & Nygren, 2014).

References

Anderson, C. (2018) *Apostles of Certainty: Data Journalism and the Politics of Doubt*. Oxford: Oxford University Press.

Ananny, M., & Crawford, K. (2015) A liminal press: Situating news app designers within a field of networked news production. *Digital Journalism*. 3(2), 192–208.

Appelgren, E. (2018) An illusion of interactivity. The paternalistic side of data journalism. *Journalism Practice*. 12(3), 308–325.
Appelgren, E., & Nygren, G. (2014) Data journalism in Sweden: Introducing new methods and genres of journalism into 'old' organizations. *Digital Journalism*. 2(3), 394–405.
Ausserhofer, J., Gutounig, R., Oppermann, M., Matiasek, S., & Goldgruber, E. (2017) The datafication of data journalism scholarship: Focal points, methods, and research propositions for the investigation of data-intensive newswork. *Journalism*. Epub ahead of print April 4.
Bell, E. J., Owen, T., Brown, P. D., Hauka, C., & Rashidian, N. (2017) *The Platform Press: How Silicon Valley Reengineered Journalism*. Tow Center for Digital Journalism, Columbia Journalism School. Available from: https://academiccommons.columbia.edu/doi/10.7916/D8R216ZZ [Accessed 18 September 2018].
Bochannek, A. (2012) Have you got a prediction for us, UNIVAC? *Computer History Museum Curatorial Insight*. Available from: www.computerhistory.org/atchm/have-you-got-a-prediction-for-us-univac/ [Accessed 9 July 2018].
Boczkowski, P. J. (2004)˙*Digitizing the News: Innovation in Online Newspapers*. Boston, MA: MIT Press.
Boczkowski, P., & Papacharissi, Z. (eds.). (2018) *Trump and the Media*. Cambridge, MA: MIT Press.
Borges-Rey, E. (2016) Unravelling data journalism: A study of data journalism practice in British newsrooms. *Journalism Practice*. 10(7), 833–843.
Borges-Rey, E. (2017) Towards an epistemology of data journalism in the devolved nations of the United Kingdom: Changes and continuities in materiality, performativity and reflexivity. *Journalism*. Epub ahead of print February 1. DOI: 10.1177/1464884917693864
Boyles, J. L., & Meyer, E. (2016) Letting the data speak: Role perceptions of data journalists in fostering democratic conversation. *Digital Journalism*. 4(7), 944–954.
Broersma, M. (2010a) Journalism as performative discourse: The importance of form and style in journalism. In: Rupar, V. (ed.). *Journalism and Meaning-Making: Reading the Newspaper*. Cresskill, NJ: Hampton Press, pp. 15–35.
Broersma, M. (2010b) The unbearable limitations of journalism: On press critique and journalism's claim to truth. *The International Communication Gazette*. 72(1), 21–33.
Callison, C., & Young, M.L. (Forthcoming) *The View from Somewhere: The Limits of Journalism*. New York: Oxford University Press.
Chadwick, A. (2013) *The Hybrid Media System: Politics and Power*. Oxford: Oxford University Press.
Christensen, C. M., Raynor, M. E., & McDonald, R. (2015) What is disruptive innovation. *Harvard Business Review*. 93(12), 44–53.
Christensen, C. M., Skok, D., & Allworth, J. (2012) Breaking news: Mastering the art of disruptive innovation in journalism. *Nieman Reports*. 66(3), 6–20.
Coddington, M. (2015) Clarifying journalism's quantitative turn: A typology for evaluating data journalism, computational journalism, and computer-assisted reporting. *Digital Journalism*. 3(3), 331–348.

Coddington, M. (2019) Defining and mapping data journalism and computational journalism: A review of typologies and themes. In: Eldridge II, S., & Franklin, B. (eds.). *The Routledge Handbook of Developments in Digital Journalism Studies*. Abingdon: Routledge.

De Maeyer, J., Libert, M., Domingo, D., Heinderyckx, F., & Le Cam, F. (2015) Waiting for data journalism: A qualitative assessment of the anecdotal take- up of data journalism in French-speaking Belgium. *Digital Journalism*. 3(3), 432–446.

Deutsche Welle Innovation Blog. (2017) The #PerugiaPledge: Creating a set of guidelines for data journalists. Available from: http://blogs.dw.com/innovation/perugiapledge/

Dick, M. (2014) Interactive infographics and news values. *Digital Journalism*. 2(4), 490–506.

DiMaggio, P. (1988) Interest and agency in institutional theory. In: Zucker, L. (ed.). *Institutional Patterns and Organizations Culture and Environment*. Cambridge, MA: Ballinger, pp. 3–21.

Domingo, D. (2008) Interactivity in the daily routines of online newsrooms: Dealing with an uncomfortable myth. *Journal of Computer-Mediated Communication*. 13(3), 680–704.

Ericson, R. (1998) How journalists visualize fact. *The Annals of the American Academy of Political and Social Science*. 560(The Future of Fact, November), 83–95.

Felle, T. (2016) Digital watchdogs? Data reporting and the news media's traditional 'fourth estate' function. *Journalism*. 17(1), 85–96.

Fink, K., & Anderson, C. W. (2015) Data journalism in the United States: Beyond the 'usual suspects'. *Journalism Studies*. 6(4), 467–481.

Fligstein, N., & McAdam, D. (2011) Toward a general theory of strategic action fields. *Sociological Theory*. 29(1), 1–26.

Freelon, D., McIlwain, C., & Clark, M. (2018) Quantifying the power and consequences of social media protest. *New Media & Society*. 20(3), 990–1011.

Guess, C. (2016) In defense of old-school reporting tactics in the age of data journalism. *International Journalists' Network*, May 17. Available from: https://ijnet.org/en/blog/defense-old-school-reporting-tactics-age-data-journalism

Gynnild, A. (2014) Journalism innovation leads to innovation journalism: The impact of computational exploration on changing mindsets. *Journalism*. 15(6), 713–730.

Hacking, I. (1990) *The Taming of Chance*. Cambridge, UK: Cambridge University Press.

Hannaford, L. (2015) Computational journalism in the UK newsroom: Hybrids or specialists. *Journalism Education*, 4, (6–21).

Hermida, A. (2015) Web 2.0 and the News. In: Donsbach, W. (ed.). *The International Encyclopedia of Communication*, Vol. 12. Malden, MA: Wiley-Blackwell. https://doi.org/10.1002/9781405186407.wbiecw010.pub2

Hermida, A., & Young, M. L. (2017) Finding the data unicorn: A hierarchy of hybridity in data and computational journalism. *Digital Journalism*. 5(2), 159–176.

Howard, A. B. (2014) The art and science a-driven journalism. *Tow Center for Journalism White Paper*. Available from: https://academiccommons.columbia.edu/catalog/ac:zcrjdfn317

Karlsen, J., & Stavelin, E. (2014) Computational journalism in Norwegian newsrooms. *Journalism Practice*. 8(1), 34–48.

Knight, M. (2015) Data journalism in the UK: A preliminary analysis of form and content. *Journal of Media Practice*. 16(1), 55–72.

Küng, L. (2015) *Innovators in Digital News*. Reuters Institute for the Study of Journalism. London: IB Tauris.

Lawrence, T. B., & Suddaby, R. (2006) Institutions and institutional work. In: Clegg, S. R., Hardy, C., Lawrence, T. B., & Nord, W. R. (eds.). *Sage Handbook of Organization Studies*, 2nd Edition. London: Sage, pp. 215–254.

Lepore, J. (2014) The disruption machine: What the gospel of innovation gets wrong. *The New Yorker*, June 23, 30–36.

Lewis, S. C., & Usher, N. (2013) Open source and journalism: Toward new frameworks for imagining news innovation. *Media Culture & Society*. 35(5), 602–619.

Lewis, S. C., & Zamith, R. (2017) On the worlds of journalism. In: Boczkowski, P. J., & Anderson, C. W. (eds.). *Remaking the News: Essays on Technology and the Futures of Journalism Scholarship in the Digital Age*. Cambridge, MA: MIT Press.

Lindgren, A., & Corbett, J. (2018) Local news map data. *Local News Research Project*. Available from: http://localnewsresearchproject.ca/category/local-news-map-data [Accessed 27 August 2018].

Loosen, W., Reimer, J., & De Silva-Schmidt, F. (2017) Data-driven reporting: An on-going (r). evolution? An analysis of projects nominated for the Data Journalism Awards 2013–2016. *Journalism*. [Preprint]. https://doi. org/10.1177/1464884917735691 [Accessed 15 April 2018].

Lowrey, W. (2012) Journalism innovation and the ecology of news production: Institutional tendencies. *Journalism & Communication Monographs*. 14(4), 214–287.

Padgett, J. F., & Powell, W. W. (2012) *The Emergence of Organizations and Markets*. Princeton, NJ: Princeton University Press.

Parasie, S., & Dagiral, E. (2013) Data-driven journalism and the public good: 'Computer-assisted-reporters' and 'programmer-journalists' in Chicago. *New Media and Society*. 15(6), 853–871.

Patru, D., Lauche, K., van Kranenburg, H., & Ziggers, G. W. (2015) Multilateral boundary spanners: Creating virtuous cycles in the development of health care networks. *Medical Care Research and Review*. 72(6), 665–686.

Peters, C., & Broersma, M. (2014) Introduction: Retelling journalism: Conveying stories in a digital age. In: Broersma, M., & Peters, C. (eds.). *Retelling Journalism*. Walpole, MA: Peeters. Groningen Studies in Cultural Change, Vol. 49, pp. ix–xix.

Picard, R. (2014) Twilight or new dawn of journalism? Evidence from the changing news ecosystem. *Digital Journalism*. 2(3), 273–283.

Picard, R. (2016) Submission to the House of Commons Standing Committee on Canadian Heritage, Local Media Inquiry, Email Sent to Mary Lynn Young, October 1.

Public Policy Forum. (2017) *The Shattered Mirror: News, Democracy and Trust in the Digital Age*. Available from: https://shatteredmirror.ca/wpcontent/uploads/theShatteredMirror.pdf

Rogers, S., Schwabish, J., & Bowers, D. (2017) *Data Journalism in 2017: The Current State and Challenges Facing the Field Today*. Google News Lab.

Royal, C. (2012) The journalist as programmer: A case study of the New York Times interactive news technology department. *ISOJ Journal*. 2(1), 5–24.

Royal, C., & Blasingame, D. (2015) Data journalism: An explication. *#ISOJ*. 5(1), 24–46.

Singer, J. B., Domingo, D., Heinonen, A., Hermida, A., Paulussen, S., Quandt, T., Reich, Z., & Vujnovic, M. (2011) *Participatory Journalism: Guarding Open Gates at Online Newspapers*. Malden, MA: John Wiley & Sons.

Skelton, C. (2018) There are fewer journalists in Canada than 15 years ago: But not as few as you might think. *J-Source*, May 4. Available from: http://j-source.ca/article/canadian-journalists-statistics/

Stalph, F. (2018) Classifying data journalism. *Journalism Practice*. 12(10), 1332–1350.

Stencel, M., Adair, B., & Kamalakanthan, P. (2014) *The Goat Must Be Fed*. Duke Reporters' Lab, the DeWitt Wallace Center for Media & Democracy.

Tabary, C., Provost, A. M., & Trottier, A. (2016) Data journalism's actors, practices and skills: A case study from Quebec. *Journalism*. 17(1), 66–84.

Taylor, J. (2016) Nate Silver has a Donald Trump problem: Where does data journalism go now? *Salon.com*. Available from: www.salon.com/2016/05/15/nate silver has a Donald Trump problem where does data journalism go now/ [Accessed 25 July 2018].

Usher, N. (2016) *Interactive Journalism: Hackers, Data, and Code*. Urbana, IL: University of Illinois Press.

Winseck, D. (2016) Media and Internet concentration in Canada report 1984–2015. *Canadian Media Concentration Research Project*. Available from: www.cmcrp.org/media-and-internet-concentration-in-canada-report-1984-2015/

Witschge, T., Anderson, C. W., Domingo, D., & Hermida, A. (2018) Dealing with the mess (we made): Unraveling hybridity, normativity, and complexity in journalism studies. *Journalism*. First published March 22.

Young, M. L., & Hermida, A. (2015) From Mr. and Mrs. Outlier to central tendencies: Computational journalism and crime reporting at the Los Angeles Times. *Digital Journalism*. 3(3), 381–397.

Young, M. L., Hermida, A., & Fulda, J. (2018) What makes for great data journalism? A content analysis of data journalism awards finalists, 2012–2015. *Journalism Practice*. 12(1), 115–135.

2 Data journalism in liquid times

On a Saturday morning, the Chicago Marriott Downtown hotel was inundated with a particular kind of journalist. The hotel was hosting more than a thousand journalists who in some shape or form work with data to research, find and tell news. They were attending the 2018 Computer-Assisted Reporting (CAR) conference, organized by the Investigative Reporters & Editors (IRE) and the National Institute for Computer-Assisted Reporting (NICAR). Traditionally the annual stomping ground for investigative reporters, the conference has gradually shifted its focus towards data, attracting a broader range of journalists.

Over the past decade, the number of journalists from the U.S. and around the world attending the event has more than tripled. In 2008, attendance was at just under 300 (Stiles, 2017). By the time of the 2018 conference, the number was above a thousand, lured by its promise to "offer everything from the basics on using spreadsheets, databases and online mapping to data visualization and the latest technological advances" (IRE, n.d.). Speakers ranged from experienced investigative reporters, data reporters, interactive developers to academics in computational journalism. The rise in attendees points to the increasing interest in data journalism in the profession and the spread of data journalism into the everyday roles of journalists, as well as the expansion of the field to include more non-traditional actors. As Fink and Anderson suggested, "data journalism, it appears, is everywhere" (2015: p. 1), noting the increased industry buzz and scholarly interest around the phenomenon. In a seemingly fast-growing field, the question is "whether and how data journalism actually exists as a thing in the world" (Fink & Anderson, 2015: p. 1).

Data journalism encompasses blurred and porous definitions of journalism involving data. It covers overlapping and divergent organizational titles and responsibilities. It embodies a fluidity of roles and employment. And it includes continuously developing tools, technologies and platforms. As a field of study, the domains offer a lens to examine the issues facing scholars and professionals in an emergent field where fluidity is a defining element in journalistic processes, practices, positions and products. It contrasts with more delineated and defined roles and responsibilities in earlier mediums such as print and broadcast. The debate over the nature of data journalism, who is a data journalist and what counts as excellence in data journalism, is far more than an exercise in academic discourse. It speaks to the fact that fields in a state of flux create opportunities to contest epistemologies, expertise, economics and ethics in journalism (cf. Lewis & Westlund, 2015), opening ways for new actors to emerge and exercise agency and/or for established actors to reassert power and authority.

Understanding liquidity in journalism

In this chapter, we consider data journalism within the framework of liquid journalism. The term was first used by Deuze (2008) to differentiate digital journalism from its earlier analogue versions. For Deuze, what has been happening in journalism is associated with the "liquid modernity" of contemporary society as defined by Polish social theorist Zygmunt Bauman (2000), where a state of flux is inherent in modern life. Karlsson defines liquid journalism as an "erratic, continuous, participatory, multi-modal and interconnected process that is producing content according to journalistic principles" (2012: p. 388). Widholm argues that "the on-going liquidization of journalism has posed long-lasting methodological problems for media researchers as most analytical models are based on static rather than dynamic methods for data gathering" (2016: p. 25). Other scholars have surfaced instead the tensions between stability and instability given the transformation of journalism, suggesting that "the phenomenon of online news production and the study of it are at a kind of liminal moment between tradition and change" (Mitchelstein & Boczkowski, 2009: p. 563).

These issues have been largely considered in the context of the analysis of online news content, given the ephemeral and temporal condition of digital news practices and routines. Data journalism shares and extends the challenges of the liquidization of journalism as data has become a growing area of journalistic practice with what Fink and Anderson say is an "explosion in data journalism-oriented scholarship" (2015: p. 322). The result has been what Coddington has described as a "flurry of research over the past decade, often overlapping and occasionally contradicting each other in its rush to document and understand a rapidly emerging phenomenon" (2019: p. 225). The inconsistencies and ambiguities from the rush to map out the contours of data journalism are inherent to research in an area that defies neat categorization.

Considering data journalism as liquid means it is possible to see, touch and feel it. But grabbing hold of it, as well as determining how data journalism flows across space and time, is another matter. The complications of conducting research in the digital realm were identified as early as 2001 by Wellman. He noted that "an Internet year is like a dog year, changing approximately seven times faster than normal human time" (Wellman, 2001: p. 2034). The challenge for social science research, including in journalism studies, is operating in "Internet time." Karpf argues that "'Internet Time' is a subject grudgingly acknowledged in our research designs, rather than incorporated within them" (2012: p. 640).

Standard research practices are ill-suited to operating in dog years, given the time lag between grant proposals, data gathering and analysis, writing, peer-review and publication. For example, in his 2012 paper, Karpf highlights books and articles published in 2011 based on data from 2006. Perhaps it is time to paraphrase Wellman: a research year is the opposite of a dog year, changing seven times slower than normal human time. Imagine, then, the complications for a field like data journalism, experiencing an explosion in both practice and research. As a form of liquid journalism, it is hard enough to pin down, let alone trying to do so in rapid, fast-flowing waters. This chapter unpacks the interrelated challenges to conducting research in a field with blurred and fluid contours, roles, titles and technologies, where different professional interpretations and activities are indicators of professional renegotiation and regeneration. As such, data journalism acts as a microcosm to consider the twists and turns of journalism as a whole, and what it means to be a journalist today.

Capturing the essence of data journalism

The very term, data journalism, embodies the contested nature of the field, surfacing how definitional terms can become an arena to assert authority. Definitions are an indication of the epistemology of data journalism, setting the parameters of the "*rules, routines and institutionalized procedures* that operate within a social setting and decide the form of the knowledge produced and the knowledge claims expressed [or implied]" (Ekström, 2002: p. 260, emphasis in original). One of the first uses of the term, data journalism, came in 2008 when *Guardian* news editor Simon Rogers used it to describe how the development team had produced software that took raw data and represented it on a map. "It's data journalism – editorial and developers producing something technically interesting and that changes how we work" wrote Rogers, editor of *The Guardian Datablog* (2008). A decade later, a Google search for the term brought up 778,000 results, while a search on Google Scholar results in 4,130 hits.

Data journalism has become an umbrella term to reference the use of data, computers and software and computational mindset in journalism. Simply asking what is data journalism surfaces the many ways in which it is practiced and understood in different professional contexts. There is also no shortage of synonyms used by professionals and scholars to talk about data journalism. A group of researchers in Austria resorted to using nine different search terms in their attempt to capture the range of publications on data journalism – from journal articles to industry reports (Ausserhofer et al., 2017). As well as using the phrase of data journalism, they also referenced data-driven journalism, data-driven reporting, computer-assisted reporting, database journalism, quantitative journalism, computational journalism and algorithmic journalism.

Journalists and editors may have an idea of what it is, but are unlikely to come up with a consistent definition. The specifics of the data journalist are colored by the interpretations of different stakeholders who have particular aims in the use of the nomenclature. Instead, professional definitions tend to be all-encompassing, framing data journalism as anything that involves reporting with data towards journalistic ends. The first chapter of the *Data Journalism Handbook*, published in 2012, seeks to answer the question of what is data journalism by saying "it is journalism done with data" (Bradshaw, 2012: p. 2). Then it adds, "but that doesn't help much" given the "troublesome terms" of data and journalism (Bradshaw, 2012: p. 2).

Asking journalists in Canada to define the phenomenon yields a multitude of answers that signal the positionality of the interviewees. Among the few things that journalists working in the area could agree on was that it involved data and storytelling, often linked to investigative reporting and the public interest. For a journalist at a regional newspaper who made a name for himself as a data journalist, it was "any type of journalism that is based on structured data, data that is rows and columns, fields and records" (Interview 11, September 18, 2015). A senior editor at a national outlet was more expansive, saying that data journalism was about "telling stories using raw data, analyzing raw data whether it's from a spreadsheet, or from a database, or from a report, finding patterns that emerge, using visualizations that might actually show a story that exists that wouldn't otherwise" (Interview 5, September 22, 2015). Another also spoke of the importance of identifying patterns. "It's very fluid, it can include quite a bit, basically anything where you're looking at a pattern of numbers whether that means numbers or events even . . . it's analyzing for patterns, essentially" she said (Interview 15, March 26, 2015).

While data sets were seen as fundamental, others highlighted the centrality of storytelling to data journalism. "It's not just good enough to count. You must tell a story at the end of the day" said a reporter at a regional newspaper (Interview 1, September 29, 2015). The importance of the story emerged in other comments. "It's using data to either, sometimes to find a story, to support a story, and ultimately on the presentation side, to effectively present that information to our audience in a way that they can, that doesn't cloud the subject matter, but actually lets them see conclusions and come to those conclusions" explained a journalist at the Canadian public broadcaster (Interview 7, September 5, 2015).

Those with a history of working with data wondered whether labels served any purpose. The National Institute for Computer-Assisted Reporting (NICAR) suggests that there is little new in data journalism. In the About section on its website, it notes that "the term 'computer-assisted reporting' was used widely in the last two decades to describe what many now call 'data journalism,'" (About, NICAR, no date). An experienced investigative reporter at a national print outlet argued "all these names are somewhat incomplete and nebulous." He recalled that "when I started doing this was a long time ago and we called it computer-assisted reporting, which was never really a good name because we don't say notebook-assisted reporting or, you know, voice-recorder assisted reporting. It's just a tool" (Interview 4, March 25, 2015). Another print reporter wondered whether a definition mattered. "I don't feel like I need to have a definition of data. You sort of know data when you see it. You know it's relevant information that's organized in some you know fairly convenient fashion" he said (Interview 10, March 25, 2015).

What emerges from interviews with journalists working in the field is a somewhat expansive definition rooted in telling stories with data (see Howard, 2014), though the specifics in their language reveal a strategic positioning in the profession on the newshound to techie spectrum (Borges-Rey, 2017). More experienced reporters tended towards definitions that aligned and reinforced with existing newsroom hierarchies and traditions, while others sought to define new spaces for themselves. Numerous studies have adopted a similar qualitative approach that show how journalists end up defining data journalism on their own terms and in ways consistent with their experience and/or professional context (Fink & Anderson, 2015; Appelgren & Nygren, 2014; Karlsen & Stavelin, 2014; De Maeyer Libert, Domingo, Heinderyckx & Le Cam, 2015).

For Swedish journalists, it was about "a set of work methods used to make journalistic sense of raw data" (Appelgren & Nygren, 2014: p. 403). But the study also surfaced a degree of confusion, with journalists with little experience in data journalism contesting whether it was a thing in itself. One Swedish journalist admitted: "I have answered your survey, but I have to admit that I do not understand the difference between data journalism and journalism in general" (quoted in Appelgren & Nygren, 2014: p. 400). Another respondent wondered what was special about data journalism, given that "data and statistics have always been a part of a reporter's work role" (quoted in Appelgren & Nygren 2014: p. 400). Such comments show how some seek to downplay whether data journalism challenges existing ways of working and knowing in journalism.

The results of a study of journalists in French-speaking Belgium showed similar tensions with journalists offering a wide range of meanings (De Maeyer et al., 2015). For example, there was disagreement over whether data visualization counted as data journalism. For some it was a simulacrum of journalism, while for others it was integral to storytelling (De Maeyer et al., 2015). Here again is a strategic positioning at play within actors in the profession with regard to a newer form of journalism that is heavily influenced by a discipline from outside, that of information visualization. The range of professional orientations around data surface in Usher's (2016) study on news interactives. She identifies a range of professional subspecialties connected in some way to data journalism. While she recognizes data journalists as those who are primarily oriented towards data, she also identifies other professional subsets who engage with data – hacker journalists, programmer journalists and interactive journalists (Usher, 2016).

Beyond trying to pin down what constitutes data journalism, there are also differences over how far it is a new phenomenon or simply old wine in new bottles. These differences are symptomatic of questions of power and agency within the newsroom as emerging norms and practices come up against established routines and conventions. A journalist at the public broadcaster in Canada suggested that what was new were the tools and the buzz. "It's become really sexy" he said, "everybody's lusting after it, but it's nothing new" (Interview 7, September 5, 2015). Even Simon Rogers, who pioneered data journalism at the *Guardian*, argues that data journalism is not as novel as it might seem, noting that "the very first *Guardian* . . . in May 1821 contained a table of data" (Rogers, 2013: Kindle edition location 299).

Such perspectives point to the genealogy of data journalism as a quantitative form of journalism (Coddington, 2015, 2019) that combines elements of continuity and change. It has its professional and epistemological roots in the use of social science methods to analyze quantitative data using computers, pioneered by Philip Meyer, who described this approach as precision journalism (Meyer, 2002). Coddington (2015) helpfully breaks down the phenomenon into three quantitative journalistic forms that capture the evolution of the application of data in journalism over time. He identifies computer-assisted reporting, data journalism and computational journalism as distinct approaches that have intersecting and diverging values and practices:

> CAR is rooted in social science methods and the deliberate style and public-affairs orientation of investigative journalism, data journalism

> is characterized by its participatory openness and cross-field hybridity, and computational journalism is focused on the application of the processes of abstraction and automation to information.
>
> (Coddington, 2015: p. 337)

Each of these distinct quantitative journalistic forms comes with its own ways of knowing, skill sets and values that can be mapped to understandings of professional identities. Borges-Rey (2017) breaks these down into two epistemological frameworks that complement and build on Coddington's typology. There is the "newshound," who approaches data within traditional journalism norms and practices, and is closely identified with CAR. At the other end of the spectrum is the "techie" who "designates an emergent journalistic approach to data based on more computational logics and mindsets" (Borges-Rey, 2017: p. 2). The "techie" approach is more closely aligned with computational journalism, at opposite end of the spectrum of data journalism.

The essence of a data journalist

Fluidity over time emerges as a key factor when it comes to identifying the practices that delineate the quantitative turns in journalism highlighted by Coddington. A body of research has sought to define journalism as practice by focusing on the features, norms and routines that characterize newswork (see, for example Tuchman, 1978; Gans, 1979). Practices are both consistent and challenged as new journalistic formats emerge over time. Tensions over overlapping and blurred roles and responsibilities in data journalism mirror past debates. In the mid-2000s, there were heated squabbles in the profession and academy over blogging as it shifted from an activity practiced outside of institutional media to a practice adopted by professionals to become a new genre in journalism (Domingo & Heinonen, 2008).

The development of data journalism at one of our sites of research, the *Globe and Mail*, reflects how practices can shift from the periphery to the center. In his memoir, the newspaper's former editor-in-chief John Stackhouse writes about how, from the late nineties, a unit called "Globe Information Services and its corps of engineers and business builders who had little to no contact with the newsroom" (2015: p. 66) published stock charts, calculators and corporate databases online. At the time, Stackhouse was a correspondent-at-large for the paper. The team was in a separate building from the newsroom. Stackhouse recalled that it accounted for three-quarters or more of traffic to the *Globe's* website, while the newsroom was producing journalism "reported, written and designed as if the newspaper era could slide smoothly into the digital age" (2015: p. 67). By 2018, what Stackhouse describes as "a new form of content" (2015: p. 67) has become commonplace at the *Globe and Mail*, with 34 people in a visual journalism team as part of the newsroom that worked on data, as well as photo, video, design, graphics and interactives across all platforms.

The make-up of the visual journalism team at the *Globe* indicates the challenges of pinning down the practices that constitute data journalism. Instead, "it's part of a lot of people's job" explained Matt Frehner, head of visual journalism (2018), encompassing digital design to development to interactives, and ranging from quick, daily charts and graphs to more extensively researched investigative projects. In this case, new and fluid professional identities have emerged as part of the reorganization of the newsroom at the *Globe*.

A similar picture emerges from studies on the practices and performativity of data journalism, with a range of ontological interpretations. In the Netherlands, data journalism was framed as a way of "upgrading journalism" (Bakker, 2014: p. 603), whereas in Norway it was "a continuation of journalistic work practices" (Karlsen & Stavelin, 2014: p. 44). In the U.K., a content analysis of leading national daily and Sunday newspapers found that data was an element in only a fraction of stories, so that "crunching data have become no more remarkable, or important, than any other form of journalism" (Knight, 2015: p. 70). In contrast, another U.K. study interviewed data journalists working across a range of media concluded that data had become part and parcel of news practices (Borges-Rey, 2016). Such research indicates how, in some contexts, data journalism has integrated into established journalistic practices.

Further muddying the waters is the professional labeling of the people involved in data journalism. Labeling can be considered a surrogate of authority, signaling a journalist's place in the newsroom hierarchy, as well as indicators of strategic positioning. In our 2015 study of Canadian journalists, titles tended to combine technological descriptors such as interactive, mobile, digital, web and data, together with more fixed professional categories such as editor, producer, coordinator, manager and developer (Hermida & Young, 2017). Among the titles were interactive editor, senior web coordinator, senior editor for mobile and interactive news, interactive developer, manager of digital products or simply, reporter.

A journalist at a broadcast organization remarked that her title was so generic as to be "a very meaningless, vague, job title" (Interview 15, March 26, 2015). An experienced data journalist expressed a degree of discomfort with his professional title. "My byline at the moment says investigative reporter, which is flattering, but not all of our work is classically investigative" he said. "But some of it is, so it's either a little embarrassing or kind of cool depending on the day" (Interview 3, September 5, 2015). The challenge of integrating newer roles within existing structures is reflected by the experience of the CBC. It recently hired four people who would take on the role and responsibilities of data journalists. But, as an editorial developer at the public broadcaster noted, they cannot officially be called data journalists as "under the union structure, they're labelled as senior reporters and they were hired according to their skill sets" (Interview 14, June 28, 2018).

The fluid nomenclature created a degree of autonomy over the construction of job titles, creating a space for journalists to self-define their position and status. At times, professional labeling as a data journalist was self-generated, evolving at times opportunistically at the individual level. For example, a journalist at a legacy print outlet noted that his "official title is based on what is written in the contract so technically I've always just been a reporter. But I started putting data journalist on my emails and nobody stopped me, so that's what I identified myself with" (Interview 11, September 18, 2015). A senior journalist at the public broadcaster noted that he was a producer, even though he considers himself a data journalist, has authored books on the topic and has taught it for many years. Instead he suggested that the term "data journalist" would be one that "hopefully we won't have to use in the future because with the prevalence of open data, with the enormity, with the availability . . . that this is a tool that everyone should have" (Interview 18, June 8, 2018).

The range of professional labels shows up in other research that has sought to map out the new roles and identities of data journalism across organizational and national contexts. For example, in a study of data journalism in the U.S., titles included specific labels such as database editor, interactive news editor and computer-assisted reporting specialist as well as more generic ones such as city hall reporter and assistant editor (Fink & Anderson, 2015). What emerge are contested and fluid relationships between traditional notions of journalistic identity, professional practice and skills that create opportunities for reinterpretation of roles and responsibilities.

Identifying the data journalist

Liquid professional labeling poses its own challenges for studying data journalism by examining the actors, practices and interactions that come together to form what we call data journalism. For researchers, it can be, as one Canadian data journalist put it, "like finding another unicorn in the middle of the woods" (Interview 14, March 26, 2015). Finding the unicorn can mean casting a wide net to capture journalists broadly working with data. For our research (Hermida & Young, 2017), the sampling of the interviewees was achieved through looking for journalists who were producing works of data journalism. It drew on previous research on data journalism in Canada, unpublished work by Canadian academic Lisa Lynch on data journalism and an industry presentation by journalist David Weisz (2012) that listed 11 data journalists in the country. Using snowball sampling, the list was then supplemented by additional referrals by our initial subjects. Such a broad and open-ended approach responds to the mutable roles and identities that have emerged in the different national media and organizational contexts.

Snowball sampling treads a fine line between representative and replicable research and an informal method of reaching a targeted sample. It is usually employed to access "hidden" populations that are hard to reach, such as vulnerable or stigmatized groups (Atkinson & Flint, 2001). Data journalists can be seen as a hidden population within the newsroom whose cohesion emerges from shared socio-discursive practices of diverse actors (see Chapter 3). Snowball sampling has been widely used to access groups who self-identify as data journalists, much as such methods are valuable to study the lives of those outside of mainstream social science research.

A study in the French-speaking part of Belgium started off by talking to professionals who attended a workshop on data journalism (De Maeyer et al. 2015). The sample was then expanded to include those mentioned in the interviews. A similar approach was used by Borges-Rey (2017) in his study of data journalism in the devolved nations of the U.K. He used a combination of Internet searches for data journalists and data-driven stories with asking subjects about other data journalists working in the area. For their study of data journalism in the U.S., Fink and Anderson (2015) looked at staff job titles, conducting searches on Google, following up on bylines on data projects and asking editors for referrals.

The strength of such broad methods lies in enabling people working in this area to define how they envision and demarcate what it means to be in data journalism through qualitative interviews. It is particularly pertinent in a fluid field, where diverse actors and their diverse interpretations signal how they interpret what is data journalism. Semi-structured in-depth interviews have become the most common method to study data journalism (Ausserhofer et al., 2017). Such methods provide a means to access and assess perspectives of the evolving field of data journalism, tapping into a growing interrelatedness in this domain. But some researchers seem to have a blind spot when it comes to critically assessing the impact of research design on findings. In their review of the literature on data journalism, Ausserhofer et al. noted that "responses of interviewees are presented as facts without acknowledging that some degree of idealization is inevitable" (2017: p. 18).

There is a risk here in relying on a self-identified group to define itself and the boundaries of what it does, given that they may seek to present what they do and its significance in the most positive light. Relying on one group to refer researchers to others can reinforce such tendencies. It introduces a selection bias in the research design whereby findings are shaped by pre-existing networks and relationships, particularly in an emergent area where so many practitioners are involved in extra-institutional activities and communities (see Chapter 3). Moreover, there is a risk that some figures in positions of relative authority in the field could exercise an undue influence over the selection of subjects (Atkinson & Flint, 2001). Research design plays a significant role, given the contested fluid space of data journalism, with its competing professional identities and epistemologies.

The question of replicability is further complicated by a precarity of roles and employment. A Canadian journalist at the public broadcaster acknowledged that “it’s a very mobile field and I think we’re likely to see a lot of people essentially create their own niches within it” (Interview 6, March 26, 2015). The community of professionals working in the field of data journalism seems to be far more transient than in other areas of journalism. In our study of Canadian data journalists, a third of the sample had changed roles or employers during the 12-month research period (Hermida & Young, 2017). One was reassigned to general reporting duties, another took a buy-out, while one moved from Canada to the U.S. The inconsistency and precarity of employment in the newly developing research field of data journalism presents significant challenges for a scholarly enterprise working in Internet time (Karpf, 2012).

The mutability of technologies

The volatility in data journalism extends to the environment in which journalists operate, considering the wider context of the technologies of content creation (see Chapter 2). In other words, journalism is a process of assemblage made up of “the interlocking material, cultural, and practice-based underpinnings of data journalism” (Anderson, 2015: p. 353). The material turn serves to acknowledge the range of actors involved in data journalism, specifically the tools, technologies and platforms implicated in newswork. But researching the influence of the materials on the processes and production of data journalism presents significant challenges given the fluidity of digital tools, technologies and platforms.

Our study of data projects in Canada highlighted the volatility surrounding the production and publication of data journalism (Young, Hermida & Fulda, 2018). A number of technical issues affected the usability of a number of our sample of 26 Canadian data journalistic projects published between 2012 and 2015. At the time of our analysis, a dynamic map on a project on welfare fraud published in 2013 by *Le Journal de Montreal* did not fit within the frame of the webpage. The frame cut off the right-hand side of the map on a desktop browser, with the loss of details of the research and production team.

In another case, a MapQuest map on school scores published by the *Hamilton Spectator* in 2014 showed up as colored dots against a gray background due to a change in the company's API. Changes in Google's mapping API also meant a 2012 data project by students at Kings College mapping 911 calls to police in Halifax no longer showed any data. Perhaps most dramatically, several projects were no longer available online. An online text story published by the *Windsor Star* linked to interactive graphics on a defunct free Wordpress-hosted site. Two data projects by students included in our initial analysis no longer existed online. One brought up an Apache testing page, while the other seemed to be a spam site in Japanese.

By July 2018, there were problems with the data visualizations in 16 of the 26 projects in our Canadian sample, making it impossible to conduct the study again. The results from Canada point to the issues when it comes to capturing online data journalism projects. It is questionable how far it would be possible to replicate similar studies. For example, the study of data projects in Quebec between 2011 and 2013 by Tabary et al. (2016), the 31 submissions to Nordic data journalism awards by Appelgren (2018), the 225 projects nominated for the Data Journalism Awards from 2013 to 2016 analyzed by Loosen, Reimer and De Silva-Schmidt (2017) or the 44 examples of award-winning data journalism from 2013 to 2016 examined by Ojo and Heravi (2018).

Journalism's liquidity online raises methodological problems not just for data journalism but for approaches reliant on static, rather than dynamic, content. The methodological challenges raised by the nature of digital news production practices were the focus of a 2016 special issue of *Digital Journalism*. In it, various scholars proposed approaches to capture the liquidity of routines that allow for the constant publication and republication flow of news content virtually in real-time around the clock (Boumans & Trilling, 2016; Karlsson & Sjøvaag, 2016; Karlsson & Strömbäck, 2010; Widholm, 2016).

Data projects are to a certain extent immune to the ephemeral and fleeting characteristics of online news as they tend to be produced over a period of time. Immediacy is not the issue. Rather it is the pace of change of a technology industry characterized by a constant cycle of updates. "Google always changes their APIs and then things break" noted the head of visual journalism at the *Globe and Mail*, Matt Frehner (2018). He acknowledged the importance from a legacy perspective of keeping projects available online for as long as possible. "This is a huge problem in visual journalism online" he added, "you don't have any projects from before 2015" explaining how some earlier work was no longer available online. It's hardly surprising, then, that two of the four Globe projects in our sample dated 2012 and 2013 were broken.

The issue is further complicated by the use and, at times, dependence on third party, and often free, tools, from Google Fusion Tables and Maps to Tableau Public (see Chapter 4). The use of easy-to-use or free tools, particularly in less well-resourced newsrooms, emerges as a theme in similar studies (Fink & Anderson, 2015; Loosen, Reimer, & De Silva-Schmidt, 2017). Just in our study, there were problems with half of the data visualization projects produced by Canadian regional newspapers. The mutability of technologies over time, coupled with a lack of dedicated tools, combines to underscore the precarity of data journalism as an object of study.

Conclusion

The challenges of researching data journalism serve as a lens to examine broader issues within journalism studies. As this chapter has illustrated, data journalism is far from a unitary form of journalism. As Coddington suggests, "data journalism is both new and old, professional and marginal, participatory and exclusive, static and shifting" (2019: p. 234). The fluidity of the field as a subset of journalism research has given rise to at least four distinct but related typologies over three years (Coddington, 2019). As Zelizer has argued, "journalism has always been multiple, multi-dimensional, multi-directional and multiply-faceted" (2009: p. 1). The discourse over the definition of data journalism, over who is a data journalist and over what constitutes data journalism mirror earlier (and ongoing) boundary debates in the profession and academy over what is journalism. The deinstitutionalization of media and the increased availability of interactive tools have fueled discussion over how to identify what is and isn't journalism. As this chapter has explored, conflict and contention over the participants, the practices and the professional norms and values of journalism (Carlson, 2015) are articulated in the realm of data journalism.

The study of data journalism, then, is the study of journalistic agency and power within an organizational context undergoing technological adaptation and balancing established and emergent media logics. The normative and epistemological tensions are indicative of strategies to assert the legitimacy and credibility of data journalism as a form of knowledge production. Anderson examines these tensions through a rich exploration of the genealogy of data journalism in the U.S., tracing how the practice relates to journalistic efforts "to render their knowledge claims more certain, contextual, and explanatory" (2018: p. 1). For his part, Borges-Rey (2017) places these tensions in a continuum from "newshound" closely aligned with investigative, computer-assisted reporting, to "techie" aligned with the use of computational approaches.

The perspectives coming from the practitioners themselves tend to rely on what sociologist Robert Park called "synthetic knowledge." This is a form of tacit knowledge "embodied in habit and custom, as opposed to analytic and formal knowledge" (Park, 1940: p. 672). Given contested perspectives on what is data journalism, one way of looking at the tacit knowledge of data journalism is through the lens of awards. Studies in this area have suggested there may be a settling on what constitutes excellence in data journalism given the prominence of investigative, data-driven projects that align with a newshound mentality (Loosen, Reimer & De Silva-Schmidt, 2017; Ojo & Heravi, 2018; Young, Hermida & Fulda, 2018). Such work points to the tensions given deeply engrained institutional values and the emergence of new actors in the newsroom with newer expertise and identities, opening the way for struggles over status, power and resources.

Studies from the perspectives of the actors seeking to assert what data journalism is and its significance are valuable in establishing the groundwork for research on an "unruly object of study" (Coddington, 2019: p. 234). They capture "who is inside and outside, who may speak, who may not, and who has authority and may be believed" (Marvin, 1998: p. 4). But they also point to the limitations of established methods to analyze fluid and mutable domains such as data journalism "where innovation proliferates, where group boundaries are uncertain, when the range of entities to be taken into account fluctuates" (Latour, 2005: p. 11).

Research on data journalism needs to contend with it as a liminal space, where "a set of field level relationships among actors who may not self-identify as journalists but nonetheless define the conditions under which news is created and circulates" (Ananny & Crawford, 2015: p. 193). Such relationships are not necessarily limited to the newsroom or actors associated with a centralized space for news production. Instead the liquidity of data journalism forces scholars to go "beyond the usual suspects" (Fink & Anderson, 2015: p. 467) and trace the actions and interactions of a range of multiple and interrelated players, practices and platforms. The messiness of data journalism is indicative of the interplay of power and agency in an emerging domain with its multiple definitions, contexts and functions.

References

Ananny, M., & Crawford, K. (2015) A liminal press: Situating news app designers within a field of networked news production. *Digital Journalism*. 3(2), 192–208.

Anderson, C. W. (2015) Between the unique and the pattern. *Digital Journalism*. 3(3), 349–363. DOI: 10.1080/21670811.2014.976407

Anderson, C. W. (2018) *Apostles of Certainty: Data Journalism and the Politics of Doubt*. Oxford: Oxford University Press.

Appelgren, E. (2018) An illusion of interactivity. The paternalistic side of data journalism. *Journalism Practice*. 12(3), 308–325.

Appelgren, E., & Nygren, G. (2014) Data journalism in Sweden: Introducing new methods and genres of journalism into 'old' organizations. *Digital Journalism*. 2(3), 394–405.

Atkinson, R., & Flint, J. (2001) Accessing hidden and hard-to-reach populations: Snowball research strategies. *Social Research Update*. 33(1), 1–4.

Ausserhofer, J., Gutounig, R., Oppermann, M., Matiasek, S., & Goldgruber, E. (2017) The datafication of data journalism scholarship: Focal points, methods, and research propositions for the investigation of data-intensive newswork. *Journalism*. [Preprint]. Available at https://journals.sagepub.com/doi/10.1177/1464884917700667 [Accessed 15th April 2018].

Bakker, P. (2014) Mr. Gates returns: Curation, community management and other new roles for journalists. *Journalism Studies*. 15(5), 596–606.

Bauman, Z. (2000) *Liquid Modernity*. Cambridge: Polity.

Borges-Rey, E. (2016) Unravelling data journalism: A study of data journalism practice in British newsrooms. *Journalism Practice*. 10(7), 833–843.

Borges-Rey, E. (2017) Towards an epistemology of data journalism in the devolved nations of the United Kingdom: Changes and continuities in materiality, performativity and reflexivity. *Journalism*. Epub ahead of print, February 1. https://doi.org/10.1177/1464884917693864 [Accessed 15th April 2018].

Boumans, J. W., & Trilling, D. (2016) Taking stock of the toolkit: An overview of relevant automated content analysis approaches and techniques for digital journalism scholars. *Digital Journalism*. 4(1), 8–23.

Bradshaw, P. (2012) What is data journalism? In: Gray, J., Bounegru, L., & Chambers, L. (eds.). *Data Journalism Handbook*. Sebastopol, CA: O'Reilly.

Carlson, M. (2015) The many boundaries of journalism. In: Carlson, M., & Lewis, S. C. (eds.). *Boundaries of Journalism: Professionalism, Practices and Participation*. Abingdon: Routledge, pp. 1–18.

Coddington, M. (2015) Clarifying journalism's quantitative turn: A typology for evaluating data journalism, computational journalism, and computer-assisted reporting. *Digital Journalism*. 3(3), 331–348.

Coddington, M. (2019) Defining and mapping data journalism and computational journalism: A review of typologies and themes. In: Eldridge II, S., & Franklin, B. (eds.). *The Routledge Handbook of Developments in Digital Journalism Studies*. Abingdon: Routledge, pp. 225–236.

De Maeyer, J., Libert, M., Domingo, D., Heinderyckx, F., & Le Cam, F. (2015) Waiting for data journalism: A qualitative assessment of the anecdotal take-up of data journalism in French-speaking Belgium. *Digital Journalism*. 3(3), 432–446.

Deuze, M. (2008) The changing context of news work: Liquid journalism for a monitorial citizenry. *International Journal of Communication*. 2, 18–36.

Domingo, D., & Heinonen, A. (2008) Weblogs and journalism. *Nodicom Review*. 29(1), 3–15.

Ekström, M. (2002) Epistemologies of TV journalism: A theoretical framework. *Journalism*. 3(3), 259–282.
Fink, K., & Anderson, C. W. (2015) Data journalism in the United States: Beyond the 'usual suspects'. *Journalism Studies*. 6(4), 467–481.
Frehner, M. Journalist (Personal communication, 2 May 2018).
Gans, H. (1979) *Deciding What's News*. New York: Pantheon.
Hermida, A., & Young, M. L. (2017) Finding the data unicorn: A hierarchy of hybridity in data and computational journalism. *Digital Journalism*. 5(2), 159–176.
Howard, A. B. (2014) *The Art and Science of Data-Driven Journalism*. New York, NY: Tow Center for Digital Journalism. Available from: http://towcenter.org/wp-content/uploads/2014/05/Tow-Center-Data-Driven-Journalism.pdf [Accessed 15 July 2018].
IRE. (no date) *2018 CAR Conference*. Available from: www.ire.org/events-and-training/event/3189/ [Accessed 15 June 2018].
Karlsen, J., & Stavelin, E. (2014) Computational journalism in Norwegian newsrooms. *Journalism Practice*. 8(1), 34–48.
Karlsson, M. (2012) Charting the liquidity of online news: Moving towards a method for content analysis of online news. *International Communication Gazette*. 74(4), 385–402.
Karlsson, M., & Sjøvaag, H. (2016) Content analysis and online news: Epistemologies of analysing the ephemeral Web. *Digital Journalism*. 4(1), 177–192.
Karlsson, M., & Strömbäck, J. (2010) Freezing the flow of online news: Exploring approaches to the study of the liquidity of online news. *Journalism Studies*. 11(1), 2–19.
Karpf, D. (2012) Social science research methods in Internet time. *Information, Communication & Society*, 15(5) 639–661.
Knight, M. (2015) Data journalism in the UK: A preliminary analysis of form and content. *Journal of Media Practice*. 16(1), 55–72.
Latour, B. (2005) *Reassembling the Social: An Introduction to Actor-Network-Theory*. Oxford: Oxford University Press.
Lewis, S. C., & Westlund, O. (2015) Big data and journalism: Epistemology, expertise, economics, and ethics. *Digital Journalism*. 3(3), 447–466.
Loosen, W., Reimer, J., & De Silva-Schmidt, F. (2017) Data-driven reporting: An on-going (r). evolution? An analysis of projects nominated for the Data Journalism Awards 2013–2016. *Journalism*. [Preprint]. https://doi.org/10.1177/1464884917735691 [Accessed 15 April 2018].
Marvin, C. (1998) *When Old Technologies Were New*. Oxford: Oxford University Press.
Meyer, P. (2002) *Precision Journalism: A Reporter's Introduction to Social Science Methods*, 4th Edition. Oxford: Rowman & Littlefield.
Mitchelstein, E., & Boczkowski, P. J. (2009) Between tradition and change: A review of recent research on online news production. *Journalism*. 10(5), 562–586.
NICAR, About Page (no date). Available from: www.ire.org/nicar/about/ [Accessed 15 June 2018].
Ojo, A., & Heravi, B. (2018) Patterns in award winning data storytelling: Story types, enabling tools and competences. *Digital Journalism*. 6(6), 693–718.

Park, R. E. (1940) News as a form of knowledge: A chapter in the sociology of knowledge. *American Journal of Sociology*. 45(5), 669–686.

Rogers, S. (2008) Turning official figures into understandable graphics: At the press of a button: Inside the Guardian Blog. *The Guardian*, December 18. Available from: www.theguardian.com/help/insideguardian/2008/dec/18/unemploymentdata [Accessed 12 June 2018].

Rogers, S. (2012) Anyone can do it: Data journalism is the new punk: Guardian Datablog. *The Guardian*, May 24. Available from: www.theguardian.com/news/datablog/2012/may/24/data-journalism-punk [Accessed 12 June 2018].

Rogers, S. (2013) *Facts Are Sacred*. London: Faber and Faber.

Stackhouse, J., (2015) Mass Disruption: Thirty Years on the Front Lines of a Media Revolution. Toronto: Random House Canada.

Stiles, M. (2017) Charting NICAR attendance, over the years. *The Daily Viz*. February 24. Available from: http://thedailyviz.com/2017/02/24/charting-nicar-attendance-over-the-years/ [Accessed 29 August 2018].

Tabary, C., Provost, A. M., & Trottier, A. (2016) Data journalism's actors, practices and skills: A case study from Quebec. *Journalism*. 17(1), 66–84.

Tuchman, G. (1978) *Making News: A Study in the Construction of Reality*. New York: The Free Press.

Usher, N. (2016) *Interactive Journalism: Hackers, Data, and Code*. Urbana, IL: University of Illinois Press.

Weisz, D. (2012) Data journalism in Canada: Why we're so far behind (and what we can do to change that). In: *Information Resource Management Association of Canada Meeting*, November, Vol. 21. Available from: www.irmac.ca/1213/2012nov.php

Wellman, B. (2001) Computer networks as social networks. *Science*. 293(5537), 2031–2034.

Widholm, A. (2016) Tracing online news in motion: Time and duration in the study of liquid journalism. *Digital Journalism*. 4(1), 24–40.

Young, M. L., Hermida, A., & Fulda, J. (2018) What makes for great data journalism? A content analysis of data journalism awards finalists 2012–2015. *Journalism Practice*. 12(1), 115–135.

Zelizer, B. (2009) Introduction: Why journalism's changing faces matter. In: Zelizer, B. (ed.). *The Changing Faces of Journalism: Tabloidization, Technology and Truthiness*. London: Routledge.

3 Strength in numbers*

Canada's largest national newspaper, the *Globe and Mail*, has been recognized nationally and internationally for a powerful 2017 data #MeToo era journalism series, titled "Unfounded," that has been seen by many to represent the future of journalism, and data journalism, specifically. The *Globe's* Editor-in-Chief, David Walmsley, called the series a "global benchmark" in the promotional article that accompanied the announcement that it won the Global Editors Network Data Journalism Awards competition award for investigation of the year (Katawazi, 2017). A *Globe* article described the series as shedding light "on a significant abuse of power or failure to uphold the public interest," referencing feedback from the GEN awards judges (Katawazi, 2017). The *Globe* described the series' contribution and impact in its submission to the Online News Association awards as,

> the result of a 20-month-long investigation into how police forces handle sexual assault cases. The *Globe* sent 250 freedom-of-information requests to every Canadian police service, requesting data for both sexual assault and physical assault. Our data team exhaustively and meticulously analyzed, parsed and re-reported the raw responses. What they found was damning: Police dismiss 1 in 5 sexual assault claims as baseless. Within a week, police forces serving more than 1,000 communities had launched investigations into more than 10,000 sexual-assault complaints.
>
> (ONA, 2017)

On the day after the series won another national award, a tweet by Matt Frehner, head of Visual Journalism at the *Globe*, was liked 111 times (by 13 June) linking the award to financial support for journalism in Canada. "When people ask, 'why should I pay for @globeandmail?' This is why. This is the team that worked on the original 20-month Unfounded investigation. Journalism that matters takes time, money and unflagging commitment"

(Frehner, 2018). The tweet included a screen grab of credits for 27 people involved in the series from reporting and writing to data reporting and analysis, photography, design and editing. The broad range of people on the project reflects the phenomenon of collaboration, both formally and informally, in data journalism. This chapter explores how collaboration is displacing competition in formal projects that engage actors from different disciplines and formerly separate parts of the newsroom such as news, advertising and sales, as well as informal and formal exchanges between journalists working for competing news outlets.

The *Globe* team that worked on the series explored reports of sexual assault referred to as unfounded by police services in Canada, meaning the allegations had been dropped because no legal violation had been determined and "no further action taken" (Roberts, Johnson & Grossman, 2009: p. 228). Methodologically they focused on a number of questions related to sexual assault including but not limited to the number of sexual assault complaints, sexual assault charges and the number of unfounded complaints in police jurisdictions across the country (Doolittle, 2017b). They obtained the data after filing almost 250 freedom of information requests yielding data from 873 police jurisdictions (Doolittle, Pereira, Blenkinsop & Agius, 2017). The series used basic descriptive statistics to identify an unfounded rate for sexual assaults in Canada – which was 19.39 per cent over a five-year period – significantly higher than the rate for other crimes as well as the rate of false reports (Doolittle, 2017a). The series conforms to general forms, norms and epistemologies for investigative journalism and previous studies of data and award-winning journalism, in that it exposes an important public issue to affect the policy agenda, contains a combination of specialized genres and human interest sources.[1] The series begins with an emotional personal anecdote to draw the reader into the story.

> The keg party was a 10-minute walk from Ava's new home. . . . Her first big bash as a university student. . . . Somewhere along the line, she isn't sure when, she found herself talking to a guy from the party. . . . She remembers they were outside and kissing. And then she blacked out. When things came back into focus, Ava says, she was on the ground near a pine tree, at the north side of the house. She was naked and cold and lying in the dirt. The man was inside of her.
>
> (Doolittle, 2017a)

Ava's allegation of rape and its subsequent dismissal by the local police became one of the many unfounded reports of sexual assault identified by the series. As requisite in digital and data journalism, the series included data visualizations, charts and numerous digital genres, including video, text and a searchable interactive map to allow audience members to find the unfounded rates of their local police force. The series was so exceptional that journalists we interviewed at competing news organizations talked about it as the "bar we all strive to meet," with discussions about major projects in the pipeline as "maybe this will be our Unfounded" (Interview 14, June 29, 2018).

But what is different in this important public service award-winning series to denote its articulation as data journalism, both an emergent and rebranded category of journalism and award categories since 2012? How does this series differ in its norms and practices from other journalism genres defined by systematic research, such as investigative journalism and other longer-form journalism genres across media? As we discuss in previous chapters, the definition of data journalism is still developing, ranging from approaches that have tried to distinguish this subfield as a set of unique forms, practices, processes, professional roles and identities (Borges-Rey, 2017; Coddington, 2019; Usher, 2016). Data journalism is seen in part as continuity from CAR and investigative journalism, and in part as change with respect to its reliance on "data" and computational methods, genres and logics with impacts on professional identities and epistemologies including norms, practices, performativity, materiality, reflexivity and power – articulating along a continuum of approaches from "newshound" to "techie" (Borges-Rey, 2017: p. 2). Any attempt at a thorough definition according to Borges-Rey (2017), "would require normalizing tensions between the competing ontological features displayed by a variety of journalistic methodologies that deal with data" (p. 2).

While we address continuity and change in other chapters including methods and identities, this chapter is focused on one significant shift in the nature of journalism reporting and writing; the collaboration required for data projects. A team of eight journalists was identified as responsible for the Unfounded series in the award story, while nine journalists are referenced on the lead story for the series (Doolittle, 2017a). Matt Frehner (2018), who leads the *Globe's* visual journalism and data lab, describes what he calls a "bespoke" data journalism unit at Canada's largest national newspaper organization as the organizational structure behind the series and other data journalism at the news organization. What started as an "interactive news team" in 2014, grew to eight editors and coders in 2015, is now the Visual Journalism team with 34 reporters, analysts, editors listed on the website as of July 2018 – the largest of its kind in Canada. This group includes professional designations that span traditional technology, content and business domains of the newsroom. Under the heading, Data and Visual Journalists, the team is described on the website as a "cross-disciplinary group of editors, designers, developers, photographers, videographers and graphic artists" (*Globe and Mail*, no date).

Ojo and Heravi's (2018) study of award-winning data journalism submissions to the Global Editors Network (GEN) is illustrative of this organizational cultural shift in journalism. They find the majority of winners require a team of people with data expertise in a range of domains from computation and programming to data analysis and visualization. In a separate study of data journalism practices across 43 countries globally, Heravi (2017) found that 46 per cent of newsrooms had a dedicated data team, with most newsrooms (70 per cent) employing data teams of anywhere between one and five people to a small elite group (5 per cent) boasting 15 people or more. This internal cooperation is in addition to external collaborations with academics, consultants and other journalists through professional affiliations and networks (Hermida & Young, 2017; Hewett, 2017; Young & Callison, 2017). According to Borges-Rey (2016), collaboration is one of the areas that data journalists are innovating in service of quality journalism, which is constructed as more trustworthy and credible content:

> Data journalists have also innovated by institutionalizing a whole new range of norms and conventions to both legitimize their practice, and overcome generalized public mistrust of journalism. In this respect, data journalism uses methods reinforced by values such as numeric infallibility, scientific rigor, computational neutrality, crowdsourced collaboration, intra-and extra-newsroom co-operation, and hyperlocal empathy to generate exclusives that are generally perceived as more accurate and transparent.
>
> (p. 842)

Our early research in 2015 identified the growth of cooperation among a range of people in newsrooms. One of the main themes that emerged during our interviews about changes in norms and practices activated by data journalism was a mindset of increased collaboration rather than competition that went beyond formal structures and institutional media constructs. Several interviewees mentioned the scarcity of journalists working with data, particularly in Canada, which facilitated the need for collaboration. "Because it's such a small group and we kind of know everybody and we . . . all came up together doing this this type of work, it's very collaborative," said one journalist (Interview 17, December 17, 2015). Another noted "there can't be more than a dozen in the country. So when they find each other, it's like finding another unicorn in the middle of the woods" (Interview 14, March 26, 2015).

The urge to work together in a small increasingly specialized domain grounded in open-source principles has been found in other studies of data journalists globally (Borges-Rey, 2017; De Maeyer, Libert, Domingo, Heinderyckx & Le Cam, 2015; Parasie & Dagiral, 2013) as well as works of journalism such as the Panama Papers. But what does this collaborative impulse signal for the field and profession, which has been rooted in a competitive economic and sociological context for so long (Ehrlich, 1998; Lacy, 1989, 1992; Young, 2005)? The notion of disruptive innovation is one way that technological change is being understood in journalism. It has infiltrated organizational narratives and become perceived as a necessity for success bolstered by time-pressured binary futures of adapt or be left behind. It is an insufficient model, however, to make sense of the complexities of change occurring within the various systems of journalism – the hybridity of news forms and practices, technological adaptation and its social construction, in addition to "understanding the role of actors in effecting, transforming and maintaining institutions and fields" (Lawrence & Suddaby, 2006: p. 215). Indeed, it falls short to explain the strategic action of groups or occupational subspecialties as Usher (2016) refers to data journalists and other interactive journalists to what could be considered multiple crises in the journalism ecosystem (Fligstein & McAdam, 2011).

We draw from recent frameworks for understanding organizational change from organizational and institutional sociology. Our contribution is to see change as less focused on singular economic disruptions, and more of a constant process of change and conflict, with field shifts attuned to strategic actors (including technologies), their abilities within the system and specific environmental externalities (Fligstein & McAdam, 2011). We argue that data journalists are at the coalface of the most current journalism crises, and charting their response allows a data point to understand 20 years of technology-fueled journalism. They represent a history of continuity of systematic research from CAR and investigative journalism, and consistent professional ideology of exposing important public issues for the public, as well as emergent cultural, political and sociological practices that draw on values of sharing, expanding expertise and ways of knowing in journalism that intersect with journalist-technologist cultures.

Their ascendance in well-funded journalism organizations in Canada is in part a function of the political economics of a highly concentrated news industry where journalists are more concerned with their declining power (PPF Report, 2017). In addition, there are impacts from outside players such as increasingly powerful audiences and platforms (which we address in an earlier chapter) that are in part reconfiguring understandings of the need for intra organization and/or industry competition. In the process, data journalists are growing in power, strategically and performatively reframing their relative roles, identity and potentially the field of journalism in the process to respond to concerns about shifting power relations and the relative value and credibility of journalism in a digital information landscape – as well as the breaking down of formerly distinct business operations relative to audiences/publics and their roles.

From "competitive ethos" to collaborative impulse

The impulse to collaborate and cooperate has been a consistent finding with respect to understanding change occurring in news norms and practices in the domain of data journalism in Canada, the U.S., U.K. and northern Europe (Borges-Rey, 2016, 2017; Hermida & Young, 2017; Lewis & Usher, 2014; Parasie & Dagiral, 2013; Royal, 2010). Borges-Rey (2016, 2017) identifies cooperation within and outside of the newsroom as well as collaboration with a range of actors as one of the newer data journalism norms being used to advance and legitimize journalism. He isolates the origin of the impulse to collaborate and/or cooperate in open source, crowdsourced principles and philosophies identified in tech and data cultures as well as the need to access specialized data skills and knowledge. His approach replicates other studies that have found that cooperation and collaboration are newer norms being incorporated within the competitive environment that has long informed the culture of legacy news norms despite evidence of some cooperation historically.

In the U.S., three studies (Parasie & Dagiral, 2013; Royal, 2010; Young & Hermida, 2015) have used qualitative interviews and/or ethnography to examine the way that data and computational journalists understand their identities and operate within mainstream newsrooms in three major cities. All found evidence of an emerging technoculture that operates through both collaboration and tension in U.S. newsrooms with specific epistemological, professional labeling and organizational impacts. Parasie and Dagiral (2013) interviewed 15 data journalists, journalism professors and advocates for open data in Chicago in 2010 and examined two corpuses of investigative journalism projects and journalism-programmer online texts. Borges-Rey (2017) summarizes their findings regarding collaboration, when he suggests that the data journalism model coalesces around and is "fostered by a progressive collaboration amongst journalists, programmer-journalists and civil actors with computing proficiency who seek to strengthen government accountability and citizen participation by releasing public data" (p. 4). In addition, he identifies further shifts that emerge from pragmatic concerns that reinforce the impulse to collaborate in order to access specialized computational skills with journalists in his study who embraced "open-source ideals" seeking "internal or external collaboration in their efforts to overcome these limitations" (Borges-Rey, 2016: p. 12).

Despite numerous sophisticated contributions to the development of data and the impact of computational thinking and practice on journalism with respect to collaboration, an etiology of the origin of what collaboration is and what it is allegedly an antidote or cure for – newsroom competition – is scarce. This gap is a relevant conceptual concern as multiple kinds of journalism competition – from sociological in terms of competitive norms and practices to economic competition between journalism organizations – have informed journalism studies since the last century. Collaboration however is emerging as a newer norm of journalism in prominent conversations about journalism in public discourse. A 2009 report by Leonard Downie and Michael Schudson titled The Reconstruction of American Journalism identified an overall trend towards collaboration among all journalists – not just data journalists:

> Reporting is becoming more participatory and collaborative. The ranks of news gatherers now include not only newsroom staffers, but freelancers, university faculty members, students, and citizens. Financial support for reporting now comes not only from advertisers and subscribers, but also from foundations, individual philanthropists, academic and government budgets, special interests, and voluntary contributions from readers and viewers. There is increased competition among the different kinds of news gatherers, but there also is more cooperation, a willingness to share resources and reporting with former competitors. That increases the value and impact of the news they produce, and creates new identities for reporting while keeping old, familiar ones alive.
>
> (Downie & Schudson, 2009: n.p.)

The "willingness to share resources and reporting with former competitors" from the Downie and Schudson report marks a significant turn from decades of literature from media economics and the sociology of news. Collaboration has also been identified as an important turn in Canada. A recent report on the state of the media for the federal government referenced partnerships and collaboration as a way to encourage growth among digital-only journalism players (Public Policy Forum, 2017).

This identification with collaboration is in contrast to historic disciplinary orientations and theoretical concerns within the Journalism Studies literature that have tended to focus on competition as an important sociological, cultural and/or economic force grounding norms, practices and economics within journalism. Competition has been found to contribute to quality journalism by encouraging financial commitment from journalism organizations (Lacy, 1992) to facilitating diversity of opinion for communities, all the while resisting the oligopolizing tendencies of news organizations.

Concurrently competition has its detractions, which includes evidence that it supports the proliferation of sensational low-cost news content (Franklin, 2008; McManus, 1994) and reinforces gendered news norms and practices (van Zoonen, 1998; Young, 2005).

Ehrlich (1997) studied competition in television newsrooms in the U.S. from a political economic perspective and found a "competitive ethos" among journalists, referencing research by organizational studies scholar Gareth Morgan. He found journalists engaged in individualist competitive practices and values that supported the political economy of television news in the latter 20th century, an era that prioritized ratings and inter-news outlet competition. Just over 20 years ago, he found that competition was such a prevailing force in newsrooms that "newsworkers and their organizations [were] consistently measuring their performance against that of selected other newsworkers and news organizations" to determine who was the best, with a "scoop" one of the main ways of winning (Erhlich, 1997: p. 304).

For Erhlich, this competitive ethos was both a sociological phenomenon exhibited in news norms and practices, and a cultural habit that created a sense of community internal to and external to journalism. It was distinct from the economics of journalism, which was trending towards oligopoly in North America. This community of competition was also involved in socializing journalists; we address the training and education component of data journalism in Chapter 5. Others have found organizational structures oriented towards gender hierarchies, with competition informing sociological and cultural understandings – in this case with a masculinist cast – of what is journalism and news, such as scoops and hard news as opposed to soft news (van Zoonen, 1998). Finally, Erhlich's research also identified evidence of collaboration. He found that journalists on specialized beats shared information among each other, speculating that "such reporters begin to identify strongly with the community of other reporters on their particular beats, perhaps even more strongly than they identify with their respective news organizations" (1997: p. 312).

"Strategic action fields"

That competition and collaboration are implicated in our understanding of journalism organizations is not surprising given research from organizational sociologists such as Fligstein and McAdam (2011) who study organizational fields to understand organizational change and collective action. They blend a number of approaches including social movement theory and Bourdieu's theory of fields, to build a coherent theory of organizational change oriented around what they call "strategic action fields" which are "concerned with the efforts of collective actors to vie for strategic advantage in and through interaction with other groups in what can be seen as meso-level social orders" (p. 2). They argue that "field stability is generally achieved in one of two ways: through the imposition of hierarchical power by a single dominant group or the creation of some kind of political coalition based on the cooperation of a number of groups. At the core of the problem is whether or not the strategic action field will be built on coercion, competition, or cooperation" (p. 17).

Their approach to organizational change is relevant to journalism as a more complicated way to understand social stability and change as opposed to the disruption model, which as we discuss in Chapter 1 was intended as an economic model in specialized cases. They posit a more general approach to change – one not solely linked to technology – in which the creation and maintenance of fields inform every organization and involve a "constant jockeying" for position with "conflict and change . . . far more common than the prevailing view of settled fields" (Fligstein & McAdam, 2011: p. 5). This approach is counter to institutional approaches that presume stability or the disruption literature from economics that charts disruptive innovations and their impact on firms and markets. They instead focus on actors in the field (incumbents/challengers), their interests, relative position, the rules and access to resources, as well as the state of the overall field.

Fligstein and McAdam identify three kinds of fields: "emerging, stable or in the process of transformation" (p. 20). The latter, also identified as "field crisis," is relevant to contemporary journalism, and is defined as "destabilization of a field that really threatens the underlying order" (p. 15). They point to three kinds of "shocks" that can initiate a crisis. The first two are also relevant to the field of journalism with the first one: "invasion by outside groups . . . that had previously not been active players in the field"[2] (p. 15). According to Fligstein and McAdam, these outside groups make the "most effective competitors because they are not bound by the conventions of the field and instead are free to bring new definitions of the situation and new forms of action to the fray" (p. 15). Technology platforms such as Facebook and Google can be considered as effective new competitors. Sylvia Chan-Olmsted, for example, talked about collaboration and "co-opetition" among legacy media and tech giants in her keynote to the 2018 World Media Economics and Management Conference in South Africa, comparing the relative core value of all of the media players. She described the emergent tech giants as making gains in the traditional legacy journalism value chain, such as content creation, yet identified them as media adolescents in this space even as they establish competitive advantage through their ability to connect with news consumers. We address the impact of technology platforms on data journalism in Chapter 4.

The second shock – which Fligstein and McAdam identify as the most common – occurs in the "form of changes in resource dependencies or changes in the pattern of interaction between providers and audiences for the inputs and outputs" of the strategic actions fields (p. 16). Here one can imagine the impact of digital technologies on previous patterns of interaction between journalism providers and audiences and/or citizens. Platforms and audiences are interconnected in the field of data journalism. Data journalists use open-source platform technologies to do their work and audience analytics are increasingly being integrated into newsrooms as a necessary expertise. Finally, this theory is helpful in a journalism context as it focuses on collective actors not issues – in our case the collective identity of data journalists.

Fligstein and McAdam therefore provide a productive framework for understanding crises – not solely the economic decline narrative fueled by technology favored by industry leaders and pundits (Siles & Boczkowski, 2012) – and strategic action within journalism, while addressing gaps in previous approaches. For example, they add to Bourdieu by moving beyond the individual to address collective response. At the same time, they acknowledge they offer tools to conceptualize how these fields "work to build and then hold their groups together in the face of struggle in a broader field" (p. 20). In the next section, we will examine how data journalists are jockeying for position within the field of journalism and coalescing around double binds around trust in journalism and its core mission that have emerged in the early 21st century.

From "service" to the future of the industry

As discussed in the introduction, our study involves an almost complete sample of data journalists in 2015 in Canada with some key interview updates in 2018. A main theme we explored in our interviews in 2015 and 2018 with data journalists and/or journalist/technologists was how much they were integrated into their respective journalism organizations. Three years ago, we largely found them positioned in "service" roles located in marketing and/or IT, contributing to journalistic output but with no writing or traditional journalism contributions and capacity. Expertise in this domain was located in lone data journalists, who functioned semi-autonomously in the newsroom. There was also a category of technologist, the freelance data wrangler, who benefitted from the emergent professional labeling and collaborative networks of data journalists, filling an expertise gap in legacy journalism organizations and extending the range of the field of interrelated actors.

This finding is similar to Borges-Rey (2016, 2017) and Parasie and Dagiral (2013), in that we found collaborations were largely the result of a demand for computational tools and knowledge, some shared epistemologies and cooperation within a small and emergent professional identity. Similar to Ehrlich's reference to collaboration among reporters on specialized beats, these data journalists came together around their professional identity and need to share information. Collaboration was facilitated in part through informal Slack groups and participation in professional associations such as NICAR. Only at two journalism organizations – one national print organization and the public broadcaster – did we find evidence of a growing technoculture with data journalists having an impact on journalism epistemologies, professional labeling and norms and practices, largely in the form of collaboration. But it was still obviously early days for all organizations.

Gaps inhibiting their integration largely emerged around professional nomenclature to describe hybrid editorial and technological positions, such as graphic design and what would have formerly been considered library research skills. An interviewee said that some of the newsrooms were "viewing us as a more modern version of a graphics department, that you can make requests of" (Interview 14, March 26, 2015). Another noted that, in the past, a librarian would be doing their work in recording and maintaining data sets. Now, though, "reporters have to curate datasets, be a librarian, seek them out, make sure the data is robust, and it's complete, test the data," (Interview 1, September 18, 2015) given the decline of librarian positions within newsrooms.

The tensions between long-standing reporters and staff with data skills were particularly evident at one of the legacy print outlets in our sample. One interviewee recalled how he faced issues over credit for his contribution to stories, particularly when it came to bylines: "Am I being treated as a reporter? Am I being treated as some other reporter's research assistant? 'Cause I'm really not that interested in that kind of role" (Interview 3, March 26, 2015). A hierarchical nature of relationships between traditional journalists and others with data or visualization skills emerged in several of the interviews. A journalist employed by a legacy print outlet with a background in computer-assisted reporting explained how he handed off his work to a graphic designer to make it visually appealing: "A good illustration next to my story, gets (a) my story better play in the paper, and (b) more people to read it. That is sadly where it starts and ends with me" (Interview 1, October 18, 2015).

At another legacy print organization, experienced journalists said they turned to data specialists who were both physically and organizationally outside of the newsroom to help with data analysis and analytics. These specialists were employed by the advertising side of the organization, but would be recognized by receiving a shared byline on the finished story. As one veteran journalist put it, "they're contributing to these stories in a meaningful way but they're not writing the words" suggesting what words were more important than numbers or images (Interview 8, March 25, 2015). Hierarchical distinctions were present but expressed differently at another national news organization. Within this institutional context, interviewees emphasized how it was necessary to prove the value of data journalism to the core of the news organization by producing original stories that could be versioned for multiple platforms. While seeing their work more as a traditional investigative team, focused on longer-term projects and outside the day to day, there was a recognition of the importance to "keep a regular churn of stories going" (Interview 15, March 26, 2015).

At the public broadcaster, there was a sense of greater openness to data journalism, with one interviewee talking about "a cultural shift in seeing the value of this, or perhaps more accurately, seeing the potential" (Interview 7, March 26, 2015). Another said that he "definitely sensed much more excitement about our work and interest to learn more about our work" (Interview 13, March 26, 2015). Members of the multimedia and interactive unit were cognizant of the importance of educating the newsroom about the potential and processes of data journalism to the extent that "we still have a lot to teach the newsroom, which I think is more on us than on them at this point" (Interview 13, March 26, 2015).

Three years later

Three years later, interviews with subjects at respected legacy news organizations suggest growth and change in the data journalism domain with respect to collaboration, professional identity and their performative power within journalism. One of the organizations we identified as showing early stage evidence of a blended technoculture has grown from a small team to a unit of 34 with an interactive data group of five or six people and many on the team with some data skills (Frehner, 2018). The Canadian Broadcasting Corporation has also expanded its number of designated data journalists to four located in regional newsrooms across the country, connected to a central programming team. Organizations in general are seeing growing interest and demand for training in data journalism in the newsroom, reflected in data journalism education, which will be addressed in Chapter 5. This increase in numbers is reflected globally with respect to the number of journalists on data teams that we reference earlier in the chapter (Heravi, 2017).

However, it isn't just the size of the team and demand that has shifted. Data journalists are participating in newer forms of collaboration, not just skills renewal, access to expertise and support for complicated projects. Journalists with data as a professional label are engaging as part of collaborative teams that come together at the story generation level where there's "more ephemeral brainstorming and project work" (Frehner, 2018) as opposed to the more traditional hierarchical journalism assignment model. At the same time, data journalism's location as central to one of journalism's main epistemological methods of finding news in data for the public good – linked to its roots in CAR and investigative journalism – is also emerging more powerfully. The Unfounded project referenced in the introduction is one such project that is seeing journalists across the country coalesce around aspirational goals of journalism in Canada.

> There has been a big push with the overlap between our team and the investigative team in doing much more data-driven investigative projects. And that is really coming to its own in the last I would say 18 months. The biggest example of that is the Unfounded project
>
> (Frehner, 2018)

This support for a prominent high impact and globally recognized journalism project in Canada is perhaps not surprising given the dearth of good news in journalism, with headlines about media more likely to be about layoffs than launches. As a country with a media landscape that includes a public broadcaster, serving multiple languages (CBC North broadcasts in eight Indigenous languages, French and English), Canada has long struggled with a media market beset with issues of concentration of journalism ownership that date back to a federal government report in 1970 and before (Winseck, 2016). According to media economist Robert Picard in a report on the state of local journalism, Canada is one of the most highly concentrated media markets globally; "levels of vertical integration are extraordinarily high compared to most other nations and horizontal integration is very high" (Picard, 2016: np).

Despite arguments that the proliferation of digital journalism content and competition is an antidote to concentration in Canada, according to Picard (2016), "the basic provision of news and information nationally, provincially, and locally remains highly constrained, and issues of diversity and pluralism in that provision remain salient." Economic competition then remains a concern in these domains. A 2017 report on the state of the media by a national non-profit think tank, the Public Policy Forum, led by a former senior journalism manager and insider, however, locates the necessary policy intervention in three other areas, with concentration of ownership not contained on the list. These areas included: "fragmentation, revenue consolidation and indifference to truth," which have "overtaken simple concentration of ownership as the main threat to holding public officials to account and reflecting Canadian society back to its citizens" (PPF, 2017: p. 3). This bind between critics, who call out the country's high level of industry concentration, and insiders, focused on maintaining journalism legitimacy, is relevant to understanding the collaboration impulse and what its impact on professional identity means for journalism and data journalism in Canada. It is pertinent to the gains these data journalists are making within journalism – even in the past few years since our first series of interviews. For example, the 2017 Public Policy Forum Report identifies government support for data journalism as necessary and part of a journalism democracy fund/initiative that we reference in Chapter 1.

Building on Usher (2016) and Borges-Rey (2017) who identify the identity building efforts of players in the data domain, we suggest that these gains in Canada are the result of strategic action of data journalists at a time of crises and contradictions about core ideals and ideologies of journalism largely around journalists' ability to be "impartial, neutral, objective, fair and [thus] credible" (Deuze, 2005: p. 447). According to Frehner, despite some remaining skepticism, data journalism is the future because of its support methods and epistemological approaches that further trust in journalism.

> There are still some pockets of skepticism about the value of data in terms of investigative reporting. But I think by and large it has become and will continue to be even more a central part of the biggest and most important work that we do. Partly and maybe almost entirely because of its connection to trust in journalism and authority in journalism in that if you can show your data, if you can show the background of your work, if you can prove without a doubt that this thing you're saying is true – that lends credibility to your site.
>
> (Frehner, 2018)

He goes on to talk about the value that data journalism – structured data – brings to journalism authority as one antidote at a time of field instability and crisis, particularly in the United States, and the "much more partisan" and "community-driven journalism that is not based in fact." For Frehner, data journalism, similar to his tweet at the beginning of this chapter is linked to an "emphasis on trust and integrity" and is

> very connected to our business model of driving subscription, driving change and improving that through data is it's all actually quite interconnected. When in the past you . . . could write out a 3,000-word story and fudge a little bit. . . . Now you write it and you say here's the data. We know. Prove us wrong.
>
> (Frehner, 2018)

He links the Unfounded series with journalism accountability, transparency and information sharing through its ability to support citizen engagement. For Frehner,

> had that story been a bit more anecdotal, been a bit more of our standard weekend feature where this is a problem, there's this clearance code etc., it would not have had the impact as here's the data – look up your own city.

The authority here, while rooted in data, is oriented towards a *newshound* mindset in terms of the purpose of journalism, with the values of transparency and sharing with the audience emergent norms. That it is occurring at one of the largest and most well-funded newsrooms in the country is consistent with our previous research and others that have identified resources and political economy as elements that affect a newsroom's ability to adapt.

Consequently, data and its open-source philosophy are having an impact on sharing information with the public largely as an antidote to contemporary contestations over journalism's ability to provide "authoritative reportage" (Waisbord, 2018). Data journalists have established a bridge between *newshound* and *techie* approaches, shifting the impulse to withhold data from audiences identified by our 2015 interviews and study of award-winning data journalism projects in Canada, which found that most projects did not share their data, towards greater transparency of method for readers and publics to interpret and assess the data behind the news. This transition is potentially a strategic value creation as Chan-Olmsted (2018) has identified newer tech competitors as better at creating community and relationships than legacy media.

Conclusion

At a time when conventional wisdom about some of journalism's foundational ideals is under siege, we find data journalists at well-funded media organizations in Canada able to take advantage of instability, contradictions and crises in the field with respect to credibility in journalism, newer competitors and a shifting relationship with the audience to advance their own professional interests, identity and community of practice. We suggest that the growth in the subcategory or genre of data journalism is at the coalface of a number of shocks in journalism, which is supporting their own competitive advantage.

We find data journalists increasingly able to use their advantaged position in the field of journalism to make inroads on long-standing norms of competition towards increased collaboration internal and external to the newsroom, while internally succeeding in their own competition for professional primacy and resources. They are able to take advantage of these crises to promote their professional identity, norms and practices, in effect potentially adding to field stability, performing what journalism and can should do in a digital and increasingly data-driven world. At the same time they are advancing their own relative position balancing the traditional and technological as they advocate for a way of understanding the field and professional ideology of journalism in a period of contested ideals and conflicting messages about journalism credibility.

Notes

* Contains excerpts from Hermida, A., & Young, M. L. (2017) Finding the data unicorn: A hierarchy of hybridity in data and computational journalism. *Digital Journalism*. 5(2), 159–176.

1 See Wahl-Jorgensen's (2012) study of Pulitzer Prize journalism winners, and Parasie and Dagiral's (2013) study of data journalism in Chicago where they find a combination of visualizations of data, charts and personal witnesses in a selection of projects, while Ojo and Heravi (2018) found that the main purpose of winning data awards stories in their study of GEN data journalism winners was to inform.

2 According to Küng, Picard and Towse (2008), "previous technological advancements in the media and communications industries prior to digitalization tended to mimic and optimize existing processes or products without altering the underlying concepts: thus early television programs were radio shows with pictures, and the wordprocessor offered enhancements to electronic typewriters. Digitalization differs from these because it allows the development of fundamentally new products, services and processes. One might conclude, therefore, that digitalization has had a more profound impact on economic and social change than the Internet itself" (p. 4).

References

Borges-Rey, E. (2016) Unravelling data journalism. *Journalism Practice*. 10(7), 833–843. DOI: 10.1080/17512786.2016.1159921

Borges-Rey, E. (2017) Towards an epistemology of data journalism in the devolved nations of the United Kingdom: Changes and continuities in materiality, performativity and reflexivity. *Journalism*, 1–18. DOI: 10.1177/1464884917693864

Chan-Olmsted, S. (2018) *Saving Journalism and Media in the Age of Tech Giants: Collaboration or Co-Opetition with the Frenemy?* [Keynote]World Media Economics and Management Conference, May 7, Cape Town, South Africa.

Coddington, M. (2019) Defining and mapping data journalism and computational journalism: A review of typologies and themes. In: Eldridge II, S., & Franklin, B. (eds.). *The Routledge Handbook of Developments in Digital Journalism Studies*. Abingdon: Routledge.

De Maeyer, J., Libert, M., Domingo, D., Heinderyckx, F., & Le Cam, F. (2015) Waiting for data journalism: A qualitative assessment of the anecdotal take-up of data journalism in French-speaking Belgium. *Digital Journalism*. 3(3), 432–446.

Deuze, M. (2005) What is journalism? Professional identity and ideology of journalists reconsidered. *Journalism*. 6(4), 442–464.

Doolittle, R. (2017a) Unfounded. *The Globe and Mail*, February 3. Available from: www.theglobeandmail.com/news/investigations/unfounded-sexual-assault-canada-main/article33891309/ [Accessed 5 June 2018].

Doolittle, R. (2017b) How the Globe collected and analyzed sexual assault statistics to report on unfounded figures across Canada. *The Globe and Mail*, February 3. Available from: www.theglobeandmail.com/news/investigations/unfounded-sexual-assault-canada-data-methodology-claims/article33891819/ [Accessed 5 June 2018].

Doolittle, R., Pereira, M., Blenkinsop, L., & Agius, J. (2017) Will the police believe you? *The Globe and Mail*, February 3. Available from: www.theglobeandmail.com/news/investigations/compare-unfounded-sex-assault-rates-across-canada/article33855643/ [Accessed 5 June 2018].

Downie, L., & Schudson, M. (2009) The reconstruction of American journalism. *Columbia Journalism Review*, November/December. Available from: https://archives.cjr.org/reconstruction/the_reconstruction_of_american.php

Ehrlich, M. (1997) The competitive ethos in Television newswork. In: Berkowitz, D. (ed.). *Social Meanings of News*. London: Sage Publications, pp. 301–317.

Fligstein, N., & McAdam, D. (2011) Toward a general theory of strategic action fields. *Sociological Theory*. 29(1), 1–26.

Franklin, B. (2008) The future of newspapers. *Journalism Practice*. 2(3), 306–317. https://doi.org.ezproxy.library.ubc.ca/10.1080/17512780802280984

Frehner, M. Journalist (Personal communication, 2 May 2018).

Frehner, M. (2018) June 12. Available from: https://twitter.com/mattfrehner/status/1006709163676848133 [Accessed 13 June 2018].

Globe and Mail. (no date) Data and visual journalists. Available from: www.theglobeandmail.com/about/journalists/data-and-visual-journalists/ [Accessed 25 July 2018].

Heravi, B. (2017) State of data journalism globally: First insights into the global data journalism survey. *Medium*, August 1. Available from: https://medium.com/@Bahareh/state-of-data-journalism-globally-cb2f4696ad3d

Hewett, J. (2017) Collaborative learning: From CAR to data journalism and Hacks/Hackers. In: Mair, J., Keeble, R. L., Lucero, M., & Moore, M. (eds.). *Data Journalism: Past, Present and Future*. Bury St Edmunds: Abramis, pp. 5–22.

Hermida, A., & Young, M. L. (2017) Finding the data unicorn: A hierarchy of hybridity in data and computational journalism. *Digital Journalism*. 5(2), 159–176.

Katawazi, M. (2017) Unfounded investigation wins international data journalism award. *The Globe and Mail*, June 22. Available from: www.theglobeandmail.com/news/national/globe-unfounded-investigation-wins-international-data-journalism-award/article35437307/ [Accessed 15 June 2018].

Küng, L., Picard, R., & Towse, R. (2008) Introduction. In: Küng, L., Picard, R., & Towse, R. (eds.). *The Internet and the Mass Media*. Los Angeles: Sage Publications, pp. 1–16.

Lacy, S. (1989) A model of demand for news: Impact of competition on newspaper content. *Journalism & Mass Communication Quarterly*. 66, 40–48. https://doi.org/10.1177%2F107769908906600105

Lacy, S. (1992) The financial commitment approach to news media competition. *Journal of Media Economics*. 5(2), 5–21.

Lawrence, T., & Suddaby, R. (2006) Institutions and institutional work. In: Clegg, S. R., Hardy, C., Lawrence, T. B., & Nord, W. R. (eds.). *Sage Handbook of Organization Studies*, 2nd Edition. London: Sage Publications, pp. 215–254.

Lewis, S., & Usher, N. (2014) Code, collaboration, and the future of journalism: A case study of the Hacks/Hackers global network. *Digital Journalism*. 2(3), 383–393.

McManus, J. (1994) *Market-Driven Journalism: Let the Citizen Beware?* Thousand Oaks, CA: Sage Publications.

Ojo, A., & Heravi, B. (2018) Patterns in award winning data storytelling. *Digital Journalism*. 6(6), 693–718. DOI: 10.1080/21670811.2017.1403291

Online Journalism Awards. (2017) 2017 general excellence in online journalism: Large Newsroom: Winner. *The Globe and Mail*. Available from: https://awards.journalists.org/entries/the-globe-and-mail-2017/ [Accessed 13 June 2018].

Parasie, S., & Dagiral, E. (2013) Data-driven journalism and the public good: 'Computer-assisted-reporters' and 'programmer-journalists' in Chicago. *New Media and Society*. 15(6), 853–871. DOI: 10.1177/1461444812463345

Picard, R. (2016) Submission to the House of Commons Standing Committee on Canadian Heritage, Local Media Inquiry, Email Sent to Mary Lynn Young, October 1.

Public Policy Forum. (2017) *The Shattered Mirror: News, Democracy and Trust in the Digital Age*. Report for Heritage Canada.

Roberts, J., Johnson, H., & Grossman, M. (2009) Trends in crimes of sexual aggression in Canada: An analysis of police reported and victimization statistics. In: Winterdyk, J., Reichel, P., & Dammer, H. (eds.). *A Guided Reader to Research in Comparative Criminology/Criminal Justice*. Bochum: Universitätsverlag Brockmeyer, pp. 219–233.

Royal, C. (2010) The journalist as programmer: A case study of the New York Times interactive news technology department. *#ISOJ: The Official Research Journal of the International Symposium for Online Journalism*. 2(1), 5–24.

Siles, I., & Boczkowski, P. (2012) Making sense of the newspaper crisis: A critical assessment of existing research and an agenda for future work. *New Media & Society*. Online First version of the article is Available from: http://nms.sagepub.com/content/early/2012/08/21/1461444812455148.abstract

Usher, N. (2016) *Interactive Journalism: Hackers, Data and Code*. Urbana: University of Illinois Press.

van Zoonen, L. (1998) One of the girls? The changing gender of journalism. In: Allen, S., Branston, G., & Carter, C. (eds.). *News, Gender and Power*. New York: Routledge, pp. 33–46.

Wahl-Jorgensen, K. (2012) The strategic ritual of emotionality: A Case study of Pulitzer prize winning articles. *Journalism.* 1–17. DOI: 10.1177/1464884912448918

Waisbord, S. (2018) Truth is what happens to News: On journalism, fake news and post-truth. *Journalism Studies*, published online July 6.

Winseck, D. (2016) Media and Internet concentration in Canada report 1984–2015. *Canadian Media Concentration Research Project.* Available from: www.cmcrp.org/media-and-internet-concentration-in-canada-report-1984-2015/ [Accessed 3 September 2018].

Young, M. L. (2005) *Crime Content and Media Economics: Gendered Practices and Sensational Stories, 1950–2000* (Unpublished doctoral dissertation). University of Toronto, Toronto.

Young, M. L., & Callison, C. (2017) When gender, colonialism and technology matter in a journalism startup. *Journalism*, First published online December 20. https://doi.org/10.1177%2F1464884917743390

Young, M. L., & Hermida, A. (2015) From Mr. and Mrs. Outlier to central tendencies: Computational journalism and crime reporting at the Los Angeles Times. *Digital Journalism.* 3(3), 381–397.

4 The materiality of data journalism*

Introduction

A Celtic symbol with three spiraling legs emerging from the center was the symbol of the company behind many large engineering projects of the 20th century, from electric power plants to railways to the facilities for the Manhattan Project. Stone and Webster adopted the triskelion as a logo to symbolize the integration of money, engineering and construction (Bijker, Hughes & Pinch, 1987). The triskelion could also serve as a symbol for data journalism to reflect the assemblage of journalism, data and technology. Much of the research on the field has focused on the first two legs of journalism and data, often exploring professional identities, forms and processes. This chapter examines the materials that make up data journalism, from data sets to tools to platforms.

Taking its cue from Anderson and De Maeyer (2015) on the materiality of journalism, this chapter considers the objects of data journalism to explore how technologies in this field are shaping, being shaped by and impacting journalism epistemology. It takes on board Schudson's critique that "too often we have 'black-boxed' an object or material thing and have thereby failed to look inside at how its active processes shape our affairs, an impact based on its specific features that, in most cases, could well have been different and might still be made different" (2015: pp. 61–62). Materiality offers a lens to understand how the tools and technologies of data journalism interact, influence and are influenced by editorial decisions and processes. The materials of data journalism, from the personal computer to Microsoft Excel to Google Maps, "generate contestation, negotiation and adaptation in thinking about what matters" (Zelizer, 2009: p. 5).

We argue that the material choices made in the selection and use of specific tools, technologies and platforms have an impact not just in how information is conveyed but in what types of topics and issues are covered, as well as what is journalism, what it can do, who does it and how it is practiced. What emerges is a material landscape in which a handful of tools and platforms exercise disproportionate power over journalistic norms and practices. There is a comparable branching when it comes to the skills and knowledge required in the technologically specific forms of data journalism.

The capacity of data journalists as strategic actors of regeneration is related to not just the technologies available, but also to ability to identify and benefit from affordances of software tools and platforms. Data journalists in well-resourced media organizations that are investing in the field have been able to leverage technologies and tools to advance new practices and conventions that enhance the journalistic imagination. In contrast, the materiality of data journalism acts as a constraining factor in newsrooms where a lack of institutional backing has contributed to a reliance on third-party, and often free, tools that require little or no training.

Avoiding techno-utopianism

Throughout its evolution, journalism has been impacted by technological innovation as novel practices develop alongside novel forms of work. As Schudson (1978) has noted, the modern, mass circulation newspaper would be inconceivable without technological innovations in printing. In the 19th century, the telegraph shortened the distance and time between an event and the reporting of it, shifting the way journalists considered what could be told in a timely manner. It served to establish what Örnebring (2010) describes as a discourse of speed that remains to this day. However, to claim the telegraph played the decisive role in the development of objectivity as a norm is to ignore broader occupational, economic and institutional factors (Schudson, 2001). The telegraph does not, in itself, force change in journalism. Rather, its impact was moderated and channeled by existing political economic, social and cultural contexts.

In any discussion of the topic, there is a risk of falling into technological determinism and approaching technology as driving social and cultural change. A more nuanced approach recognizes that technology does not, in itself, drive change, but plays a notable role in shaping and being shaped by news routines and ways of thinking. Deuze suggests that technology should be framed as an amplifier and accelerator of change, requiring a focus "on how journalists appropriate technologies in the service of established goals, strategies, and relationships in ways that accelerate current constituent trends, developments and activities of journalism" (2009: p. 82). Powers takes this further, to argue that the technologies of news production introduce what he calls technologically specific forms of work, referring "to work rooted in the affordances of technical capacities that also make claims about the journalistic nature of such work" (2012: p. 25).

Technological change does not occur in isolation nor does it predetermine outcomes. Nor is technology either neutral or revolutionary. Rather, it is historically and culturally situated, contingent on the systems within which it is deployed. New technologies develop in the context of existing practices, are tamed to align with occupational norms or are deployed as opportunities for renewal. In the context of data journalism, then, investigating the tools and technologies employed by journalists offers a lens to understand processes of appropriation, integration and adaptation. It offers a way to consider the rise of newer competences in the newsroom, such as coding and programming that are associated with emergent subspecialities of professional roles, such as the hacker journalist or programmer journalist identified by Usher (2016).

Much as the initial wave of research on online journalism was marked by a techno-utopian discourse (Steensen, 2011), so was some of the early work on data journalism. In a 2011 report drawing on interviews with nine journalists, editors and developers, Aitamurto, Lehtonen and Sirkkunen noted the growth of free or inexpensive digital tools made it much easier to analyze and visualize data. Based on the research, the team predicted a bright future for data journalism as "better tools and increased skills will make data analysis cheaper and more efficient, and this will lead to journalists discovering story topics from larger data sets, cross analyzed with other larger and larger data sets" (Aitamurto, Sirkkunen & Lehtonen, 2011: p. 16). A 2014 report on data journalism for the Tow Center for Digital Journalism went as far as predicting that "better tools will emerge that democratize data skills" (Howard, 2014: p. 72).

The shimmer of techno-utopianism among the early practitioners of data journalism comes across in a range of studies. In Chicago, programmer-journalists integrated into newsrooms brought with them an assumption that "technical artifacts [web applications, web frameworks and programming languages] hold great promise both for news organizations and democracy" (Parasie & Dagiral, 2012: p. 867). Similarly, a study of data journalism in Belgium surfaced the assumption that "progress in tools and technologies would allow easier access and processing, and would make data journalism more natural in the context of euphoria associated with new technologies" (De Maeyer, Libert, Domingo, Heinderyckx & Le Cam, 2015: p. 440).

These perspectives are consistent with the tendency of journalists to assign significant agency to the technologies that are so tightly woven with everyday newswork (Örnebring, 2010). They also suggest a tendency to idealize the nature of their work and present data journalism in the most positive light (Ausserhofer, Gutounig, Oppermann, Matiasek & Goldgruber, 2017). It is unsurprising given the fluidity of the field of data journalism (see Chapter 2), as journalists in this area have tried to assert their place in the newsroom, partly through utopian claims associated with technology.

The layers of technology

Drawing from the Science and Technology Studies literature, the technology of data journalism can be broken down into three layers (cf. Bijker, Hughes & Pinch, 1987). There is a layer of the objects of technology, from physical things such as bicycles to digital artifacts such as software. In data journalism, these include the data sets, the visuals, software and platforms. A second layer addresses the processes and activities related to a technology. These relate to the activities of data journalism, such as data scraping, analysis and visualization. Third, there is the know-how that goes into the design and manufacture of an object. These include the knowledge and skills of the journalist to wrangle, interpret and convey the data as a story. This chapter largely focuses on the first layer – the objects of data journalism – while acknowledging that these objects operate in the context of the processes and know-how of the field.

Moreover, an important distinction for journalism is that the socio-materiality of data journalism can be broken down into two broad areas – the data itself and the technological tools, innovations and platforms used to interrogate, organize and present the data. Quantitative data, from records to statistics, has a genealogy in journalism, with new forms of data objects impacting on practice. The recent rise of "Big Data," for example, "might be seen as another object of evidence that enters the journalistic bloodstream at a particular moment or moments" (Anderson, 2015: p. 351). Here, again, there is an interplay between the types of data and the use of particular technologies.

Technology has been closely associated with the three quantitative forms of journalism identified by Coddington (2015), starting with computer-assisted reporting. When Philip Meyer (2002) wrote about the application in the 1970s of social science methods to journalism, computers took up whole rooms and required a high degree of programming expertise. By the early 1990s, advances in technology had made hardware and software more accessible, greatly transforming the newsroom and the production of news (Power, 2012). Computer-assisted reporting was one of the technologically specific forms of work that grew over the late 1980s and early 1990s as distinct and separate from daily reporting.

The personal computer and its software permeated journalistic imagination at the time. By 1994, the Executive Editor of Investigative Reporters and Editors (IRE), Rosemary Armao, noted what she described as a "new strata now emerging in journalism, the reporters who know the mysteries of computers" (quoted in Powers, 2012: p. 28). Another article in the *American Journalism Review*, headlined "Baby You Should Drive This CAR," captured the idea of technological innovation driving journalism: "Now being practiced by a third generation of journalists, computer-assisted reporting, or CAR, faces a new frontier as it moves from the computer nerd in the corner to the center of the newsroom" (Ciotta, 1996: pp. 36–37). The objects of journalism – advances in the cost, size and power of computers and more user-friendly software – contributed to the emergence of CAR.

Technology didn't cause the precision journalism pioneered by Meyer. CAR emerged against a background of the journalistic movements of the 1960s in the U.S., the greater availability and demand for records and data, and the shift to introduce empirical, social science methods in journalism. It was closely tied to the ideology of journalism, with the assumption that more scientific methods would improve professional practice. Anderson notes that CAR was related to "a growing professional self-confidence on the part of journalists themselves, at least a few of whom found themselves capable of imagining an occupational world where they could operate like social scientists" (2018: p. 2).

Data journalism, the second quantitative form of journalism identified by Coddington (2015), is closely related to the advent of online journalism. Despite the haziness of the term data journalism itself (see Chapter 2), it is hard to conceive of this form of data-driven journalism without the Internet, the proliferation of free and open-source online tools, and programming techniques. Writing in 2013, Canadian investigative journalist and journalism professor Fred Vallance-Jones suggested that

> today, data have literally swept over the news business, driven partly by the emergence of a new generation of web-based technologies that have made the presentation and visualization of data-driven stories easy even for those with no database or web development experience.
>
> (2013: p. 70)

He argued that "with little more than a basic familiarity with a spreadsheet program, journalists can use online tools to make interactive maps and charts that once required significant programming skills" (2013: p. 70). The ascent of data journalism took place in a broader professional, institutional and cultural context. But it has been facilitated by easy-to-use and often free tools such as Google Maps that have removed barriers to producing works of data journalism.

Perhaps the most technologically oriented form of quantitative journalism comes in computational journalism. This form of quantitative journalism combines elements of CAR and data journalism with more computational methods and tools. Coddington defines it as "a strand of technologically oriented journalism centered on the application of computing and computational thinking to the practices of information gathering, sense-making, and information presentation" (2015: p. 335). What Bucher calls "the shaggy, emerging beast of computational journalism" (2017: p. 931) has been enabled by advances in computational hardware and software, including in automation and algorithms. Just as CAR has its roots in social science, computational journalism is "the application of computer science to the problems of public information, knowledge, and belief, by practitioners who see their mission as outside of both commerce and government" (Stray, 2011: para.2).

Fueling the interest and production of data journalism has been the increased availability of data itself against a historical background of journalists seeking to assert greater professional certainty (Anderson, 2018). Indeed, David McKie, an experienced data journalist, suggested that every reporter could practice data journalism, given "the prevalence of open data, with the enormity, with the availability, and it's just so easy to get data" (2018). Two trends are at play. One is the open data movement which advocates for making more official data more accessible to the public, often related to notions of democracy and citizen participation (Baack, 2015). The other is Big Data, which boyd and Crawford, have described as a "cultural, technological, and scholarly phenomenon" (2012: p. 663). Big Data is not just about the size of the data set as an artifact, but also the process and activities related to handling the data. Lewis and Westlund (2015) have insightfully pointed out the need to examine how big data impacts journalistic epistemology, expertise, economics and ethics.

The data set emerges as a key material artifact in the development and practice of the journalism itself, with ramifications for types of stories produced and issues covered. Our study of Canadian award winners and finalists showed that half of the data sets used in their journalism were derived from public records, with the nature of the data set shaping the focus of stories (Young, Hermida & Fulda, 2018). Completely absent were corporate data sets. Other studies have found a similar reliance on data that is publicly available or can be readily requested, coming from official bodies, research institutes or NGOs (Loosen, Reimer & De Silva-Schmidt, 2017; Tabary, Provost & Trottier, 2016). Looking at data journalism through the lens of the data set presents a reality that is at odds with the "perception that data journalism is all about massive data sets, acquired through acts of journalistic bravery and derring-do" (Knight, 2015: p. 64). Yet the data set is often the starting point for journalistic practice, and worthy of further study in and of itself to more fully understand the normative and epistemological implications for journalism.

The tools and technologies of data journalism

An analysis of the tools of data journalism reveals a continuum of technologically enhanced storytelling. An analysis of 44 examples of prize-winning data journalism projects identified more than 130 tools and frameworks

(Ojo & Heravi, 2018). The tools and approaches used were data analysis, data visualization, and web development and publishing, mapping, graphics editing, databases, data and content management and data wrangling (Ojo & Heravi, 2018). The plethora of tools indicates the fluidity of the field of data journalism, against a background of professional norms and practices, resourcing, skill sets and technologies. According to Howard, "spreadsheets were the first 'killer app' for data journalism," with database software as the "second most common tool applied in the field" (2014: p. 58). We found a wide and expanding range of tools mentioned in interviews with 18 data and computational journalists at six of the largest legacy journalism organizations in Canada, which broadly align with the three waves of data-driven journalism outlined by Coddington (2015) – computer-assisted reporting, data journalism and computational journalism. The technology also highlights the institutional "hierarchy of hybridity" identified by Hermida and Young (2017), with resourcing and tools related to broader institutional, economic and cultural factors.

The use of spreadsheets has deep roots in computer-assisted reporting. Our research found that investigative reporters with a background in computer-assisted reporting tended to rely on the spreadsheet software Microsoft Excel and the database software Microsoft Access as the workhorses of their journalism. These programs emerge as the foundation of data journalism in some interviews. David McKie, a senior investigative journalist at the Canadian public broadcaster, described spreadsheets "as the Swiss Army knife of data journalism" (2018). Excel and Access were mentioned again and again in the interviews. "I still go to Excel and Access because that's what I live and breathe," said a veteran investigative reporter at a national print outlet. "That's kind of the tools I used when I started and to a large extent that's what I still use" (Interview 4, March 25, 2015).

Microsoft software was also the tool of choice for another senior investigative journalist at a national print outlet. "Microsoft Excel, Access. Those are my two main tools for manipulating and analyzing data," he said (Interview 8, March 25, 2015). Journalists relied on these programs as they had built a depth of knowledge and level of comfort with them. An experienced data journalist who had worked in print and broadcast explained that "I use Excel a lot as I'm comfortable with Excel. Mostly what I deal with is Access to get something to the point where I can drag it into Excel 'cause then I understand what I'm doing" (Interview 3, March 26, 2015).

Some of the newer journalists tend to use a broader range of tools. The use of a smorgasbord of often free digital tools was a theme at outlets with no dedicated data development team. "There's not a single person who knows code who works in the editorial side," commented a journalist working on a daily newspaper (Interview 10, March 25, 2015). Instead he relied on

Google Fusion Tables as "that's a one-stop shop. It contains a spreadsheet database program and a visualization tool." The publication did not want to "pony up any money for additional software so you take the free version," he explained, so he turned to whatever free tools he could access online such as OpenRefine and Tableau Public.

The availability of free, open-source or inexpensive tools and platforms is largely framed as a positive element in our interviews and in other global contexts. "We love tools that don't need a developer every time to create interactive content," said Momi Peralta, data journalist at the Argentine news outlet, *La Nacion* (quoted in Howard, 2014: p. 58). Indeed, professional discourse around tools is often framed around simplifying complexity and facilitating the practice of data journalism in the newsroom. In the words of a Belgian journalist: "Any journalist could use these tools. They know how to use a computer, it's no more complicated than that" (quoted in De Maeyer et al., 2015: p. 443). Discussing the tools available in 2018, investigative journalist David McKie argued that "they've made it accessible for virtually anyone to take a piece of data, upload it to Fusion Tables or to Tableau Public, and produce a very nice interactive graph that can then be embedded into a blog post and make that story more readable on your mobile device or your iPad and get more clicks" (2018).

An absence of institutional resources or support and the reliance on a range of open and free tools is symptomatic of an institutional "hierarchy of hybridity" (Hermida & Young, 2017). Journalists in news outlets without dedicated development resources found ways of making do with whatever tools were available at little or no cost. A journalist who, at the time of the interview (March 25, 2015), was at a national newspaper listed free, open-source or low-cost software tools, including web scraping software OutWit Hub and OpenRefine to clean up data, Google Maps and Google Fusion Tables, and mapping software Mapbox. The same picture emerged at another under-resourced newsroom. "I always use Excel for pretty much any project, also Microsoft Access," said a data journalist at a national broadcaster, adding OpenRefine, Google Maps and Fusion Tables, and free data visualization programs such as Tableau Public and Data Wrapper.

The discourse on tools took on a dramatically different tone at two organizations, which had allocated or shifted resources to set up and foster robust data teams, similar to developments seen in other newsrooms (Howard, 2014; Royal, 2010). At the public broadcaster CBC, a senior news developer described how the team was taking a systemic approach to determine the needs of the newsroom and "we'll build tools to try and solve some of the problems that we identified" (Interview, March 26, 2015). At the time of the interviews, others at the public broadcaster talked about "building more tools for people to use" (Interview 13, March 26, 2015). Having a team of news developers meant the public broadcaster could use a range of programming languages on individual data projects.

Over the course of our research we noted more attention devoted to developing in-house tools at the *Globe and Mail*. By 2015, it had an interactive news team made up of editors and newsroom developers using a combination of in-house and third-party tools (Frehner & Wolfe, 2015). Among the tools built from scratch was an easy-to-use chart tool that worked across print, web, social and mobile. The head of visual journalism, Matt Frehner, described it as "a well-designed, great chart that matches our style, matches our typography, everything works and you just press export" (2018). The decision to invest in an automated in-house tool was partly driven by resource implications. It freed up graphic editors who, in the past, would spend their time producing 30 to 50 bar charts a week. "That's basically allowed us to shift from producing dozens and dozens of charts by hand," said Frehner. "Instead of 20 minutes or 30 minutes to make a chart, it takes two minutes and that's a huge time-saving" (Frehner, 2018).

The technologies adopted and adapted across the range of legacy journalism organizations in Canada are not only the result of professional identities but more significantly from the institutional context for data journalism. The norms and practices around the use of tools are tempered by the skillset of staff, resourcing within the newsroom and the organization's overall digital strategy. It is one way of assessing one of the factors identified by Lucy Küng for the success of a news organization – the "deep integration of technology and journalism because 'the future is written in code'" (2015: p. 98).

Industry and scholarly research on data journalism paint a similar picture. A roundup of the approaches used in newsrooms across the world in the *Data Journalism Handbook* illustrated the widespread use of Google tools, even in some of the larger newsrooms (Gray, Chambers & Bounegru, 2012). The volume was intended as "a useful resource for anyone who thinks that they might be interested in becoming a data journalist, or dabbling in data journalism" (Gray, Chambers & Bounegru, 2012: p. xiv). Microsoft Excel was frequently cited as a starting point to clean, organize and analyze data, together with free Google products such as Spreadsheets, Fusion Tables and Maps. "We try to pick tools that anyone could get the hang of without learning a programming language or having special training and without a hefty fee attached," explained Lisa Evans of the *Guardian*. "We're currently using Google products quite heavily for this reason" (quoted in Gray, Chambers & Bounegru, 2012: p. 161). By comparison, some of the more experienced and knowledgeable journalists mentioned more complex tools such as the coding language Python and the statistical programs SPSS and R (Gray, Bounegru & Chambers: p. 12).

The preponderance of Google tools emerged in a 2017 qualitative study of data journalism by Google News Lab. The study combined 56 in-depth interviews in the U.K., U.S., France and Germany, together with a survey of more than 900 journalists and editors. Almost half of those surveyed (426) had experience of using Google Maps. Overall, two-thirds relied on a combination of in-house and external tools, with only a fifth of data journalists using solely in-house tools and software (Rogers, Schwabish & Bowers, 2017).

A significant technological divide between well-resourced newsrooms and the rest emerges in other national contexts. A study of data journalism in Norway highlighted the use of relatively cost-effective technologies that were already available in the newsroom (Karlsen & Stavelin, 2014). Much like in Canada, these centered on Microsoft's Excel and Access, as well as free Google tools. Similarly, data journalists at smaller news outlets in the U.S. were more likely to use easily available third-party tools like Access and Excel, or free tools from Google (Fink & Anderson, 2015). In contrast, the larger and better-resourced news organizations were more likely to have developers on staff who were able to code individual projects in languages such Python or JavaScript. At a well-resourced Canadian media outlet such as the *Globe and Mail*, Matt Frehner acknowledged the advantages of using in-house tools. "I do realize that for us that's a luxury we have because we have a team that we do that with," he said (2018).

It's all about maps and charts

Overall, a review of the technologies in the field reveals how far journalists are making do when it comes to data journalism, often relying on do-it-yourself approaches that are themselves shaped by the nature of the artifacts available – from Microsoft Excel and Access to Google software. The prevalence of certain types of data visualizations used in newsrooms – maps and charts – signals how the technology used by journalists has been shaped by historical and social routines and practices in the newsroom. As journalists are required to work across mediums and be more digital, maps and charts are quick and easy ways to create visual elements for online stories.

Maps matter as often they are the most visible aspect of data journalism. Cartographic visualization representing information in a spatial domain is seemingly everywhere in data journalism. Our study of 26 Canadian projects that were finalists or winners in major data journalism awards shows a predominance of maps (Young, Hermida & Fulda, 2018). Dynamic maps were used in just over half of the sample – 14 of the 26 projects. More importantly, nine of the 14 maps relied on Google Maps. The platform provides a free and accessible methods to create dynamic maps that would otherwise require significant investment in people, training and time.

Other studies that looked at data projects through the lens of awards found a similar predominance of maps. Just under half (49.8 per cent) of the 225 projects nominated for the Data Journalism Awards from 2013 to 2016 included a map (Loosen, Reimer & De Silva-Schmidt, 2017). The results are significant as the awards handed out annually by the Global Editors Network are considered as the "gold-standard" of data journalism. Another analysis of 44 winning entries of the Global Editors Network's Data Journalism Award from 2013 to 2016 noted that most of the projects (77 per cent) used annotated graphics and maps (Ojo & Heravi, 2018).

Mapping was used in 27 out of 31 data journalism projects nominated in the Nordic Data Journalism Awards in 2013, 2015 and 2016 (Appelgren, 2018). They included 14 interactive maps, nine static ones and four map videos. The awards are considered to represent the forefront of data journalism in Nordic countries. Mapping also emerged as the data tool of choice in an earlier study of the development of data journalism at seven Swedish traditional media organizations. Maps were the go-to method to visualize data, so much so that "in almost all of the interviews the editors described maps as the standard visualizing method for data journalism projects" (Appelgren & Nygren, 2014: p. 403).

The other common form of visually representing data is charts. Bar charts are considered as "the old reliables of the field – always useful, always being used, always there when you need them" (Kirk, 2016: p. 31). In our study of award-nominated Canadian data journalism, graphs were the second most common technique used, appearing in nine of the 26 projects, second to the use of maps (Young, Hermida & Fulda, 2018). Other studies of award winners or finalists have found similar results. Static charts appeared in 60 per cent of the nominees for the Data Journalism Awards from 2013 to 2016 (Loosen, Reimer & De Silva-Schmidt, 2017). A significant number of winners of the award – 34 out of 44 – over the same period used annotated graphs and maps for interactive data storytelling (Ojo & Heravi, 2018).

The widespread use of charts goes beyond investigative, in-depth data projects. They are a regular feature of daily data-driven journalism. Bar charts were by far the most common visualization tool used on the websites of three German-language and one British legacy media organizations – *Zeit Online*, *Spiegel Online*, *Neue Zürcher Zeitung* and the *Guardian* (Stalph, 2017). Bar charts accounted for 167 out of the 510 visualizations analyzed, with maps coming in a distant second at 83. Moreover, almost half of the charts lacked any interactive features, meaning the data could not be manipulated in any way by audiences. Compared to longer-term data projects, in everyday data journalism, "bar charts remain the most accessible and easily employable data representations – particularly considering the time pressure of daily journalism practice" (Stalph, 2017: p. 15).

Easy-to-use tools influence editorial choices to create cartographic visualizations or bar charts as relatively few specialist skills are required from journalists. Moreover, both formats can be considered as a continuation of historical journalistic norms and practice. Maps have been a mainstay in print newspapers as a way of conveying visual information to readers. Monmonier argues that "as a cartographic genre, news maps reflect the objectives and values of journalistic institutions. They are timely and narrowly focused, and present highly selective views of whatever portions of the globe editors deem noteworthy" (1989: pp. 16–18). Maps provided a way to break up the monotonous gray of newsprint, particularly at a time when newspapers were facing increased competition from the visual medium of television news (Monmonier, 1989). A study in 1986 of 30 daily U.S. newspapers found that maps made up just under half of all graphics, usually to show the location of a news event (Smith & Hajash, 1988). And a survey of 125 U.S. newspapers in 1997 showed that almost all (95.9 per cent) said they regularly published maps (Utt & Pasternak, 2000). Mapping addresses one of the five Ws of journalism – the "where" of news – with the aim of helping readers understand the geographical context of a story (Griffin & Stevenson, 1994). Maps also offer journalists a way to surface patterns through the spatial representation of information, making connections that might otherwise not as apparent and revealing the story in the data (Vallance-Jones & McKie, 2017). Mapping, then, aligns with one of the key pillars of journalistic practice of identifying the geographic component of a story.

Similarly, charts have been a mainstay in print newspapers. Bar charts came second to maps in the 1986 study of U.S. dailies (Smith & Hajash, 1988) and were regularly published by two-thirds of the newspapers in 1997 (Utt & Pasternak, 2000). Much as with maps, bar charts have a long history. One of the pioneers of the field, Simon Rogers, cites an 1858 bar chart by Florence Nightingale on mortality rates among soldiers as an early example of data journalism (Rogers, 2010). In journalism, charts serve to uphold and reinforce journalistic values of objectivity and impartiality. Barnhurst (1994) points out that charts representing a seemingly neutral reality as numbers are portrayed as objective facts. He highlights that "charts are signs, not reality. They seem concrete because of the doctrine of graphic correspondence. Charts propose to represent the world first by measuring it and then by displaying those measurements in ink and space on paper" (Barnhurst, 1994: p. 36). A historical perspective highlights how easily available or free digital tools cannot simply account for the prevalence of maps and charts online, but rather they come out of broader professional conventions and practices. In fact, the affordances of technologies like Microsoft Excel and Google Maps create favorable conditions for the adoption of these two formats of displaying information.

Conclusion

While there has been a significant body of analysis and research on the "black box" aspects of digital technologies, there has been much less investigation into the black box materiality of data journalism. Philip Howard (2015), for one, has warned about the political implications of networked communication technologies, describing a world of connected devices and services that is dominated by a handful of influential actors, namely governments and large technology companies. Others, like Christian Fuchs (2017), have brought a critical lens to social media platforms, technologies and services to argue how they both structure human activity within a capitalist, profit-led informational system. These approaches consider how the complexity of the techno-social system both enables and constrains activities and outcomes.

In journalism, much of the focus of the profession and the academy has been on the increasing power of social media platforms as they relate to the hosting, filtering and monetization of news (see, for example, Bell, Owen, Brown, Hauka & Rashidian, 2017). There has been less focus on the promise and peril of the technologies, tools and services of data journalism and their impact on journalistic ways of knowing. Looking at data journalism through an STS lens on technology shows how the methods to derive meaning, and to assess the quality and validity of data are tempered by the availability of data and tools, news practices and routines and the level of skills and know-how in the newsroom. Data-driven journalism, then, can be molded by the black box effect of a range of technical artifacts which have values embedded within them from outside the field of journalism.

A review of the technologies of data journalism reveals how closely tools are associated with the layers of quantitative forms of journalism outlined by Coddington (2015, 2019). The spreadsheet, usually using Microsoft Excel, as the tool of choice in computer-assisted reporting to interrogate data, closely aligned with the practice of investigative journalism. Mapping, often Google Maps, has become the de facto way of visualizing information in data journalism. The proliferation of maps in data projects suggests that journalists may be reaching for what is possible to do given limited resources, time and training. Maps have a long history in journalism, are relatively straight-forward to produce online and do not require expert knowledge of visualization techniques. The nascent state of computational journalism means no one tool has emerged as dominant, but instead suggests that the algorithm may become the prevailing framework.

While much professional and scholarly attention is often focused on large, well-resourced news institutions, they cannot be considered as representative of the industry as a whole. As Stencel, Adair and Kamalakanthan noted in their assessment of digital technologies in the newsroom "much of the hype about digital tools and data journalism comes from the largest news organizations" (2014: p. 4). Looking at data journalism beyond elite media illustrates the shaping influence of technology. This was evident during the growth of computer-assisted reporting in the late 80s and early 90s. Larger circulation newspapers were more likely to use computers, have more journalists involved in CAR and provide training to staff (Garrison, 1999).

Given a lack of institutional, economic and social resources, free tools are an enticing choice, but they come at a cost to the journalism. In medium and small news outlets, the materiality of data journalism can end up limiting opportunities for regeneration. A lack of tools, time and know-how is evidenced in the choice of easy-to-use digital tools among newsrooms to quickly generate an interactive map. Journalistic output then is shaped less by what could be considered the best way of exploring or representing the data. It is constrained by what can be readily done for free, often using publicly available data, without the need for skills training or investment in resources. The reliance on data sets that are openly available or can be accessed from government sources such as national statistical agencies, or from research institutes and NGOs, shapes the stories and issues represented in media outlets.

Similarly, the prevailing use of third-party tools such as Google Maps is symptomatic of the issue. The mapping platform makes it easy for a newsroom to create and publish interactive, dynamic maps, without the need to invest in a team of journalists, coders and designers. The journalist learns new competences – how to produce a dynamic map – to create a long-standing product of journalism that once fell within the occupational specialty of graphic designer. Moreover, the journalist ends up playing in someone else's sandbox, according to their values and rules. The cost of free is a lifetime of software updates, unpredictable platform priorities and bewildering terms of use. For example, at the end of 2018 Google announced it was shuttering its Google Fusion Tables as of December 2019, meaning any visualizations using the tool would stop working. The journalism is inhibited by the technological limitations of the tools and colored by the values embedded in the code.

Social, economic and technological limitations and journalism norms on data journalism mean that simple interactive techniques are often used for the sake of interactivity. Every technology carries with it an assumption of how it is to be deployed. As an example, interactivity is embedded into Google Maps. The result is that a dynamic map may be used online to include an element of interactivity when a static map would have been just as effective. Such an approach gives the illusion of interactivity, which is considered one of the defining features of digital journalism (Deuze, 1999). Rather than being a genre of journalism that explores other epistemological frameworks and methods to support making meaning, data journalism becomes a means to enhance an online story with dynamic visualizations. Perceived interactivity comes due to the interplay of the three layers of technology – the artifacts of data journalism, the processes and activities associated with it and the know-how and skills needed to do it.

The technology lens highlights an emerging divide between the "haves" and the "have-nots" of the digital media revolution. The well-resourced data operations of media outlets such as the *New York Times*, the *Guardian* and the *Globe and Mail* have the ability to develop their own in-house data tools as they have the institutional means and will to invest in technology, time, training and teams. In these instances, there is an opening for individuals with the relevant expertise and competencies in these technologically specific forms of work to leverage their knowledge and bring in practices and norms from outside the field of traditional journalism. The rise of new occupational subspecialties linked to technologically specific forms of work creates opportunities for data journalists, programmers and designers to introduce and institutionalize new epistemologies of journalism given the fluidity of this space.

Note

* This chapter contains excerpts from Young, M. L., Hermida, A., & Fulda, J. (2018). What makes for great data journalism? A content analysis of data journalism awards finalists 2012–2015. *Journalism Practice*. 12(1), 115–135.

References

Aitamurto, T., Sirkkunen, E., & Lehtonen, P. (2011) *Trends in Data Journalism*. Espoo: VTT.

Anderson, C. W. (2015) Between the unique and the pattern. *Digital Journalism*. 3(3), 349–363.

Anderson, C. W. (2018) *Apostles of Certainty: Data Journalism and the Politics of Doubt*. New York, NY: Oxford University Press.

Anderson, C. W., & De Maeyer, J. (2015) Objects of journalism and the news. *Journalism*. 16(1), 3–9.

Appelgren, E. (2018) An illusion of interactivity: The paternalistic side of data journalism. *Journalism Practice*. 12(3), 308–325, DOI: 10.1080/17512786.2017.1299032

Appelgren, E., & Nygren, G. (2014) Data journalism in Sweden: Introducing new methods and genres of journalism into 'old' organizations. *Digital Journalism*. 2(3), 394–405.

Ausserhofer, J., Gutounig, R., Oppermann, M., Matiasek, S., & Goldgruber, E. (2017) The datafication of data journalism scholarship: Focal points, methods, and research propositions for the investigation of data-intensive newswork. *Journalism*. First online April 4.

Baack, S. (2015) Datafication and empowerment: How the open data movement re-articulates notions of democracy, participation, and journalism. *Big Data & Society*. 2(2).

Barnhurst, K. G. (1994) *Seeing the Newspaper*. New York: St Martin's Press,.

Bell, E. J., Owen, T., Brown, P. D., Hauka, C., & Rashidian, N. (2017) *The Platform Press: How Silicon Valley Reengineered Journalism*. Tow Center for Digital Journalism, Columbia Journalism School.

Bijker, W. E., Hughes, T. P., & Pinch, T. J. (eds.). (1987) *The Social Construction of Technological Systems: New Directions in the Sociology and History of Technology*. Boston, MA: MIT Press.

boyd, D., & Crawford, K. (2012) Critical questions for big data: Provocations for a cultural, technological, and scholarly phenomenon. *Information, Communication & Society*. 15(5), 662–679.

Bucher, T. (2017) 'Machines don't have instincts': Articulating the computational in journalism. *New Media & Society*. 19(6), 918–933.

Ciotta, R. (1996) Baby you should drive this CAR. *American Journalism Review*. 18(2), 34–40.

Coddington, M. (2015) Clarifying journalism's quantitative turn: A typology for evaluating data journalism, computational journalism, and computer-assisted reporting. *Digital Journalism*. 3(3), 331–348. DOI: 10.1080/21670811.2014.976400

Coddington, M. (2019) Defining and mapping data journalism and computational journalism: A review of typologies and themes. In: Eldridge II, S., & Franklin, B. (eds.). *The Routledge Handbook of Developments in Digital Journalism Studies*. Abingdon: Routledge.

De Maeyer, J., Libert, M., Domingo, D., Heinderyckx, F., & Le Cam, F. (2015) Waiting for data journalism: A qualitative assessment of the anecdotal take-up of data journalism in French-speaking Belgium. *Digital Journalism*. 3(3), 432–446.

Deuze, M. (1999) Journalism and the web: An analysis of skills and standards in an online environment. *International Communication Gazette*. 61(5), 373–390.

Deuze, M. (2009) Technology and the individual journalist: Agency beyond imitation and change. In: Zelizer, B. (ed.). *The Changing Faces of Journalism: Tabloidization, Technology and Truthiness*. Oxford: Oxford University Press, pp. 82–89.

Frehner, M. Journalist (Personal communication, 2 May 2018).

Frehner, M., & Wolfe, J. (2015) Inside the Globe and Mail's new interactive team. *Open News*. Available from: https://source.opennews.org/en-US/articles/inside-globe-and-mail/ [Accessed 15 January 2018].

Fink, K., & Anderson, C. W. (2015) Data journalism in the United States: Beyond the 'usual suspects'. *Journalism Studies*. 6(4), 467–481.

Fuchs, C. (2017) *Social Media: A Critical Introduction*. London: Sage.

Garrison, B. (1999) Newspaper size as factor in use of computers for newsgathering. *Newspaper Research Journal*. 20(3), 72–85.

Griffin, J. L., & Stevenson, R. L. (1994) The effectiveness of locator maps in increasing reader understanding of the geography of foreign news. *Journalism Quarterly*. 71(4), 937–946.

Gray, J., Chambers, L., & Bounegru, L. (2012) *The Data Journalism Handbook: How Journalists Can Use Data to Improve the News*. Sebastopol, CA: O'Reilly Media, Inc.

Hermida, A., & Young, M. L. (2017) Finding the data unicorn: A hierarchy of hybridity in data and computational journalism. *Digital Journalism*. 5(2), 159–176.

Howard, A. B. (2014) *The Art and Science of Data-Driven Journalism*. New York: Tow Center for Digital Journalism, Columbia University.

Howard, P. N. (2015) *Pax Technica: How the Internet of Things May Set Us Free or Lock Us Up*. New Haven, CT: Yale University Press.

Karlsen, J., & Stavelin, E. (2014) Computational journalism in Norwegian newsrooms. *Journalism Practice*. 8(1), 34–48.

Kirk, A. (2016) *Data Visualisation: A Handbook for Data-Driven Design*. London: Sage.

Knight, M. (2015) Data journalism in the UK: A preliminary analysis of form and content. *Journal of Media Practice*. 16(1), 55–72.

Küng, L. (2015) *Innovators in Digital News*. London: IB Tauris.

Lewis, S. C., & Westlund, O. (2015) Big data and journalism: Epistemology, expertise, economics, and ethics. *Digital Journalism*. 3(3), 447–466.

Loosen, W., Reimer, J., & De Silva-Schmidt, F. (2017) Data-driven reporting: An on-going (r) evolution? An analysis of projects nominated for the Data Journalism Awards 2013–2016. *Journalism*. [Preprint]. Available from: http://journals.sagepub.com/doi/abs/10.1177/1464884917735691 [Accessed 2 June 2018].

McKie, D. Journalist, CBC (Personal communication, 8 June 2018).

Meyer, P. (2002) *Precision Journalism: A Reporter's Introduction to Social Science Methods*, 4th Edition. Oxford: Rowman & Littlefield.

Monmonier, M. (1989) *Maps with the News: The Development of American Journalistic Cartography*. Chicago: University of Chicago Press.

Ojo, A., & Heravi, B. (2018) Patterns in award-winning data storytelling: Story types, enabling tools and competences. *Digital Journalism*. 6(6), 693–718. DOI: 10.1080/21670811.2017.1403291

Örnebring, H. (2010) Technology and journalism-as-labour: Historical perspectives. *Journalism*. 11(1), 57–74.

Parasie, S., & Dagiral, E. (2012) Data-driven journalism and the public good: 'Computer-assisted-reporters' and 'programmer-journalists' in Chicago. *New Media & Society*. 15(6), 853–871.

Powers, M. (2012) In forms that are familiar and yet-to-be invented: American journalism and the discourse of technologically specific work. *Journal of Communication Inquiry*. 36(1), 24–43.

Rogers, S. (2010) Florence Nightingale, datajournalist: Information has always been beautiful. *The Guardian*, August 13. Available from: www.theguardian.com/news/datablog/2010/aug/13/florence-nightingale-graphics [Accessed 21 June 2018].

Rogers, S., Schwabish, J., & Bowers, D. (2017) *Data Journalism in 2017: The Current State and Challenges Facing the Field Today*. Google News Lab.

Royal, C. (2010) The journalist as programmer: A case study of the New York Times interactive news technology department. *#ISOJ: The Official Research Journal of the International Symposium for Online Journalism*. 2(1), 5–24.

Schudson, M. (1978) *Discovering the News: A Social History of American Newspapers*. New York: Basic Books.

Schudson, M. (2001) The objectivity norm in American journalism. *Journalism*. 2(2), 149–170.

Schudson, M. (2015) What sorts of things are thingy? And what sorts of thinginess are there? Notes on stuff and social construction. *Journalism*. 16(1), 61–64.

Smith, E. J., & Hajash, D. J. (1988) Informational graphics in 30 daily newspapers. *Journalism Quarterly*. 65(3), 714–718.

Stalph, F. (2017) Classifying data journalism. *Journalism Practice*. [Preprint]. https://doi.org/10.1080/17512786.2017.1386583 [Accessed 2 June 2018].

Steensen, S. (2011) Online journalism and the promises of new technology: A critical review and look ahead. *Journalism Studies*. 12(3), 311–327.

Stencel, M., Adair, B., & Kamalakanthan, P. (2014) *The Goat Must Be Fed*. Duke Reporters' Lab, the DeWitt Wallace Center for Media & Democracy.

Stray, J. (2011) A computational journalism reading list. *Jonathanstray.com*. January 31. Available from: http://jonathanstray.com/a-computational-journalism-reading-list [Accessed 25 May 2018].

Tabary, C., Provost, A. M., & Trottier, A. (2016) Data journalism's actors, practices and skills: A case study from Quebec. *Journalism*. 17(1), 66–84.

Usher, N. (2016) *Interactive Journalism: Hackers, Data, and Code*. Urbana: University of Illinois Press.

Utt, S. H., & Pasternak, S. (2000) Update on infographics in American newspapers. *Newspaper Research Journal*. 21(2), 55–66.

Vallance-Jones, F. (2013) Making journalism better by understanding data. *Global Media Journal*. 6(1), 67–72.

Vallance-Jones, F., & McKie, D. (2017) *The Data Journalist: Getting the Story*. Oxon: Oxford University Press.

Young, M. L., Hermida, A., & Fulda, J. (2018) What makes for great data journalism? A content analysis of data journalism awards finalists 2012–2015. *Journalism Practice*. 12(1), 115–135.

Zelizer, B. (2009) Introduction: Why journalism's changing faces matter. In: Zelizer, B. (ed.). *The Changing Faces of Journalism*. London: Routledge, pp. 1–10.

5 Visualizing the future

Data journalism is quickly becoming an in-demand expertise in journalism education globally. A number of studies have identified a growing interest in data journalism education, with just over half of the journalism schools in Australia and the United States now offering courses or modules in data journalism (Berret & Phillips, 2016; Davies & Cullen, 2016; Heravi, 2018). Unlike most traditional journalism courses and streams, however, data journalism is being offered in multiple forms from programs to courses and modules in both ad hoc and more systematic ways, with increasing demand as professional development at various career stages (Heravi, 2018).

This chapter examines how data journalism expertise, its activities, products, mindsets and epistemologies, are being defined and conceptualized within journalism education, from the proliferation of data journalism courses globally to self-taught, peer learning, and workshops organized by professional organizations. We suggest that the learning opportunities in data journalism in a number of countries reflect changes in demand for training and professional development in journalism, as well as the political economy of higher education with respect to the need for growth and revenue generation from programs considered to be in high demand with students and professionals able and willing to pay for them.

The professional development literature has tended to focus on professions that require accreditation such as law, engineering and/or teaching, with limited scholarship on mid-career training in journalism aside from the lack of it and/or that journalists want more of it (Becker, Tudor, Mace, & Apperson, 2004; Cleary, 2006; Kees, 2002). A 2002 Knight report on the state of journalism education in the U.S. found that lack of training was the main source of career dissatisfaction ahead of salary and benefits, with one-third of respondents (out of a sample of almost 2,000 people) unsatisfied with professional development opportunities (Knight Foundation, 2002).

Our interviews with Canadian data journalists, in addition to other studies on data journalism education globally, suggest that data journalists are engaging in training on their own, via professional networks, online and/or gaining data journalism tools and techniques through workshops at local journalism schools (Berret & Phillips, 2016; Heravi, 2018). As soon as they become proficient enough, some are transitioning into teaching at an early stage of their career, including at least four of our interview subjects. The fact that data journalism education is proliferating beyond annual conference workshops or paid institutional training indicates that the field of journalism is changing regarding interest in skill and knowledge development throughout the course of a journalism career. According to Berret and Phillip's 2016 report on the state of data journalism education,

> Data journalism and other quantitative reporting methods, on the other hand, have been developed largely in the field. Working journalists were the ones who first saw the potential of analyzing and presenting data, and of adopting tools such as spreadsheets and databases for stories, visualizations, and apps. Much of the instruction has come through professional workshops, not in classrooms.
>
> (Berret & Phillips, 2016: p. 12)

Teaching journalism used to mean a career change or transition for journalists, whereas data journalism educators appear to be benefitting from high demand and fluidity in this space, leveraging their professional identity to add value to journalism degrees, as well as to support professional development in the field more generally. The chapter includes a discussion of a data visualization course for journalists taught by Tamara Munzner, a computer scientist and an expert on information visualization at the University of British Columbia. She co-created two visualization tools for journalists, including Overview, an open-source visual document mining application for investigative journalists, and then studied how journalists adopted the tool (Brehmer, Ingram, Stray & Munzner, 2014; Wosen, 2016). We explore how the syllabus and online course content conceptualize ways of knowing and expertise, and what these learning approaches suggest and predict about change and adaptive capacity in journalism education.

Data journalism in a global context

A number of articles has summarized the state of data journalism education in various national contexts and globally (Heravi, 2018). Scholars have looked at Australia (Davies & Cullen, 2016; Green, 2018), Canada (Leask, 2017), Europe (Hewett, 2017; Splendore et al., 2016), Hong Kong (Zhu & Du, 2018) and the United States (Berret & Phillips, 2016). They have found similar trends focused largely on calls for more data journalism education, links between data journalism and employability, laments for the lack of trained data journalism educators and consternation that quantitative skills remain underdeveloped in journalism curricula more generally. Almost all of the approaches could be considered bullish in that they advocate for data journalism education, recommending that data journalism be required and/or play a more prominent role in their relative journalism landscapes. One study published by the Tow Center for Digital Journalism headlined its section on education as Journalism Schools Rise to the Challenge (Howard, 2014), while a Knight Foundation project conducted by researchers from Columbia and Stanford universities linked a commitment to data journalism as among a set of broader changes necessary to transform journalism schools and journalism education (Berret & Phillips, 2016).

Heravi (2018) completed the only comparative study of data journalism education globally. She examined a data set of 219 global data journalism modules and/or programs representing 24 countries that she created from a list of resources assembled by Dan Nguyen, a journalist and programmer working at Stanford's Computational Journalism Lab, and supplemented by Heravi. She found that the U.S. has the greatest number of data journalism courses (148) with "data-related skills . . . now an integral part of the structure of many journalism programs in the United States" (p. 13). The next four countries with the largest offering of data journalism courses included: the U.K., Netherlands, Ireland and Australia. Seven other countries, including Canada, focused significantly on data journalism, which was defined as offering more than one module and/or a postgraduate program in data journalism (Heravi, 2018). In total, Canada had eight modules/programs in data journalism. Of all the countries surveyed, 25 universities offered full degrees or programs in data journalism.

Three other studies examine the state of data journalism education in the United States, Australia and six countries in Europe. They all take a slightly different approach to definitions of data journalism, which is reflected in their findings. Berret and Phillips (2016) interviewed more than 50 journalists, educators and students and examined 113 journalism programs in the United States, finding that 52 per cent of the programs offered an average of two data journalism classes. They concluded that data journalism's role in j-education in the United States is a narrow "set of niche practices" (p. 12). Their finding of the percentage of schools offering data journalism however could understate the impact of data journalism on U.S. curricula for reasons related to their definition of what is a data journalism course. Berret and Phillips (2016) define data journalism classes as, "focused on the intersection of data and journalism, and using spreadsheets, statistical software, relational databases, or programming toward that end" (p. 12). They excluded "courses in numeracy, research methodologies, and statistics unless they included an explicit focus on data journalism" (2016: p. 12). The decision to exclude courses that engage more traditionally with journalism method, which could be considered relevant to laddering approaches to journalism methods generally, and data journalism more specifically, suggests a narrower definition in some respects than other scholars have deployed, and affects their findings, potentially underreporting the amount of data journalism education in the United States.

Other scholars have incorporated broader and/or slightly different definitions of data journalism in their studies in addition to different kinds of courses from short to long, which makes a comparative national analysis challenging (Davies & Cullen, 2016; Splendore et al., 2016). Unlike Berret and Phillips, Davies and Cullen (2016: p. 137) incorporated "quantitative literacy"[1] as one of four main skill sets in their study of Australian universities. They found just over half of the institutions that teach journalism in Australia (53 per cent or 18 of the 34 universities) offer a range of data journalism training from complete units to more limited term activities such as lectures. From this finding, Davies and Cullen conclude that data journalism is "among the current hot topics in journalism education in Australia" (p. 144).

Splendore et al. (2016) examined data journalism education in six countries (the U.K., Italy, Germany, the Netherlands, Poland and Switzerland) at a wide range of institutions from university to vocational and associations, expanding the definition of data journalism education in their approach. They also interviewed 16 data journalism educators in 2014. They found four different kinds of institutions offering data journalism education and training. Some countries, such as Germany, the Netherlands and the U.K., saw data journalism education thriving in university settings, with market factors and competition in higher education affecting supply in all three of these countries, as well as the existence of access to information laws. Other countries saw less uptake. According to Splendore et al. (2016) in "Eastern or Mediterranean Europe, but also in highly professionalized countries like Switzerland – fully fledged data journalists only slowly enter the market, because not all media organizations are actively seeking to hire them" (p. 144). They concluded that market factors depend

> on the employability of [future] data journalists. If the media industry is able to absorb numerous data journalists, the educational system has to follow suit and train the students – often bringing together different subjects such as journalism and informatics, computing, or communication design.
>
> (p. 144)

The links identified by Splendore et al. (2016) between the political economy of the higher education context and the specific national journalism context also locate some of the motives for launching data journalism courses as similar to Chapter 3 in supporting journalism's authority and professional identity, while seeing an extension of required expertise within the field.

Definitions, learning outcomes and journalism identity

A number of distinctions and typologies have been created in the data journalism literature trying to isolate it as a coherent set of forms, practices, logics and identities from genres such as visualization to investigative to disciplinary mindsets and methodologies (Borges-Rey, 2017; Coddington, 2015; Diakopolous, 2011). We defined data journalism in our early work (Young & Hermida, 2015) as an emergent, interdisciplinary act and mindset, drawing from Diakopolous (2011), who has a PhD in computer science. He defines it as "the application of computing and computational thinking to the activities of journalism including *information gathering, organization and sensemaking, communication and presentation*, and *dissemination and public response* to news information" (Diakopolous, 2011: p. 1 *emphasis in original*).

Similar to Coddington, we drew from Wing (2006) who asserted the importance of "abstraction and automation" in understanding the contribution of computational thinking to journalism norms and practices (Coddington, 2015: p. 9). We later operationalized the definition in our study of Canadian data projects submitted to data journalism awards drawing from Coddington (2015) again, who isolates three distinct journalistic forms – computer-assisted reporting, data journalism (which includes data visualization) and computational journalism. He includes "four dimensions" to evaluate those forms: "a closed and professional vs. open and networked orientation, transparency vs opacity, epistemological orientations toward targeted sampling vs. big data, and an active vs. passive vision of the public" (Coddington, 2019: pp. 227–228).

A key tension identified by Borges-Rey (2017) and others, including in our earlier research, is whether data journalism is about continuity with respect to investigative journalism and CAR – some of the more in depth and systematic research forms of journalism – and/or is an emergent form of journalism with newer logics and methodologies, melding journalism and computer science "that explores the use of pioneering technologies in redefining the procedures of gathering, producing, presenting and disseminating news" (Borges-Rey, 2017: p. 4). We bridge that concern in this book by approaching media change through the lens of hybridity such that older and newer norms and practices are present during periods of transition (see Chapter 2).

It's perhaps not surprising then that one of the outstanding issues in the data journalism education literature relates to definitions and epistemologies, particularly the role of data. Cohen, Hamilton and Turner (2011) bring clarity to some of the reasons for this gap as they articulate the role that data performs for journalists as compared to researchers. For Cohen, Hamilton and Turner (2011), journalists view data as a process of gathering "records to address a specific question, which, when answered, marks the end of the analysis and the beginning of the story" (p. 68). They go on to compare journalists to police investigators in their approach and use of records:

> Like intelligence and law-enforcement analysts, reporters focus on administrative records and collections of far-flung original documents rather than anonymous or aggregated organized data sets. Structured databases of public records [such as campaign contributions, farm-subsidy payments, and housing inspections] generate leads and provide context sometimes documenting wrongdoing or unintended consequences of government regulation or programs. But most news stories depend as much or more on collections of public and internal agency documents, audio and video recordings of government proceedings, handwritten forms, recorded interviews, and reporters' notes collected piece-by-piece from widely disparate sources.
>
> (Cohen, Hamilton & Turner, 2011: p. 68)

This is compared to researchers and academics who "analyze comprehensive data sets of structured or unstructured records to tease out statistical trends and patterns that might lead to new policy recommendations or new marketing approaches" (Cohen, Hamilton & Turner, 2011: p. 68).

For the purposes of this chapter, Borges-Rey's (2017) typology of data journalism addresses the general disciplinary and epistemologically diverse approaches to definitions of data journalism that account for its multiple methods and logics (Coddington, 2019). He draws from a number of important scholarly studies to create a continuum that ranges from *newshound* and *techie*, showing that key scholars see data journalism along a range of methodological enhancements of existing practices to a new genre of journalism in combination with computer science.

This section examines the literature on data journalism education identifying where on the *newshound-techie* continuum data journalism courses tend to fit with respect to traditional and/or more emergent approaches, as well as what that means for the development of data journalism education. Similar to the research on data journalism that Borges-Rey examines, research on data journalism education is using definitions of data journalism in different ways from a focus on form, practices, professional identity and process with a concurrent impact on epistemology (Davies & Cullen, 2016). This range in definitions has its own challenges for comparative analysis that we explore in the next section.

Heravi's (2018) content analysis of 219 data journalism modules globally in 2018 focused on syllabi to identify the most prominent skills being taught in data education as a way to prioritize their importance to the field. She found the focus to be on process and products, with the most prominent skills involving a "complete workflow of data journalism, from finding, collecting and cleaning data, to analysis, visualization and communication," which informed 55 per cent of the courses she studied (p. 10). These courses were considered foundational, preparing "students to complete a data journalism project and produce data journalism output individually or in small groups, even if they are not using advanced tools and methods" (p. 10). The second most prominent area of education involved computer-assisted reporting (CAR) skills – all in North America – at 10 per cent of the courses examined. Heravi goes on to identify gaps, largely, advanced data analysis, indicating that "data journalism-related courses around the world overall fail to provide such courses, above the very basic statistical analysis, to their students" with coding and programing more prevalent than advanced analysis (p. 12).

Similarly, Splendore et al. (2016) analyzed data journalism courses in six countries in Europe. They observed shared learning outcomes across courses, and arrived at a definition of data journalism education similar in its focus on process and products to Heravi. They found data journalism education is "the teaching of newsmaking made by data [including all stages of the production: processing, collecting, analyzing, and visualizing data], whether it is offered by civil servants teaching journalists how to use their data or as formal courses at universities" (p. 141). Further, they found that most courses are structured by "how to collect data [both research and building up databases], analyze data [statistically] and, finally, present data [in terms of both visualization and description]" with the *New York Times* and the *Guardian* referenced as best practice examples (p. 147).

Other researchers have defined data journalism at the outset and sought to classify the nature and quantity of educational activities in a national context. For example, Berret and Phillips (2016) interviewed 50 journalists, students and educators and examined 100 programs in the United States to assess the state of data journalism. They define data journalism classes as "focused on the intersection of data and journalism, and using spreadsheets, statistical software, relational databases, or programming toward that end. We excluded courses in numeracy, research methodologies, and statistics unless they included an explicit focus on data journalism" (p. 12). Specifically they identify four domains of data journalism: data reporting, data visualization and interactives, emerging technologies such as VR and computational journalism. They found that most courses "are largely introductory, and the need is still largely for the basics, such as knowing how to use a spreadsheet, understand descriptive statistics, negotiate for data, and clean a messy data set and then 'interview' it to find a story" (p. 9). In addition, a small number (11 of 113) offered "coursework in emerging areas of data journalism, such as drones, virtual reality, and computational methods" (p. 36).

As discussed earlier, Davies and Cullen (2016) operationalized data journalism in their study of Australian universities that teach journalism with a broader focus by including quantitative literacy, as well as narrower in that they do not reference emerging technologies. They included:

> Data visualization, including how to tell stories using maps, timelines and other infographics.
>
> Quantitative literacy, including understanding sampling techniques and concepts such as descriptive and predictive statistics, significance and error margins.
>
> How to access data not obviously in the public domain.
>
> Coding and extraction of meaningful information from big data.
>
> (Davies & Cullen, 2016: p. 137)

Davies and Cullen found that most institutions in Australia teach data as visual journalism or data visualization (72 per cent) including maps, graphics and timelines. The majority used existing teaching resources in terms of faculty members, not outsourcing to other units in the university or outside of the university.[2]

Finally, a number of studies have found data journalism education and courses offered by non-traditional, sometimes interdisciplinary and/or cross departmental collaborations. Berret and Phillips single out six schools in the United States – Northwestern University, Stanford University, Boston University, Columbia University, Georgia Tech, Syracuse University – that "pair instructors for team teaching and connect journalism students with other disciplines that focus on data and computation" (p. 29). Howard mentions "a new course taught by assistant professor Meredith Broussard, a computer scientist-turned-reporter" (2014: p. 55) at Temple University. She is now at NYU Journalism.

In their study of data journalism in Chicago, Parasie and Dagiral (2013) suggest that foundations are also supporting some of the inroads of programming in journalism schools in the United States, mentioning the Medill School of Journalism as a site of collaboration with the computer science sector to support investigative journalism. These collaborations are seen to bridge disciplinary and domain differences as most of the computer scientists "do not share the statistical culture of computer-assisted reporters and have no connection with social science" but relying on "normative principles shared by open source communities and open government advocacy, they have brought in epistemological propositions of how data can support investigative journalism" (Parasie & Dagiral, 2013: p. 862). For Berret and Phillips, a benefit of these partnerships involves connecting disciplines and scholars that "share an interest in the future of technology and society,"[3] (p. 29) and they predict that data journalism education will raise the quality of journalism education as a research-oriented discipline, through data storytelling. An emerging focus in journalism education on specialization and niche programs more generally, including data journalism, computer science and big data collaborations, must also be considered as part of the current political economy of journalism education, as institutions attempt to distinguish themselves in the higher education marketplace (Knight Foundation Report, 2013).

Extended learning opportunities

While links to the profession are common in journalism education, this survey of global studies indicates an extension of learning opportunities from non-traditional education institutions as professional development. Splendore et al. point out that a number of non-university institutions are playing a "leading role" in data journalism education including free online courses (p. 147), while journalism organizations in three countries (Switzerland, Italy and the U.K.) are offering in-house training in data journalism. In the United States, Berret and Phillips found "boot camps" were popular ways to learn about data journalism coordinated by journalism organizations such as IRE/NICAR and others. The content is largely "practical, hands-on training, using data sets that journalists routinely report on, such as school test scores." They indicated that many boot camp graduates have gone on to robust data journalism careers and have also moved into teaching in journalism programs, both as adjuncts and full-time faculty, where they have integrated those teaching techniques into their classes (see also Splendore et al. for a "high conversion rate from former students to teachers" p. 145).

In Canada, Leask (2017) interviewed data journalism educators and found a trend towards self-directed online study.

> All of the participants spoke about how they had learned most of their data journalism skills in a self-directed way: through boot camps, sessions at conferences, online learning through sites like Coursera and Code Academy, or most commonly, by acquiring the skills they needed to fit a particular story they wanted to tell.
>
> (2017: p. 56)

According to one of our interview subjects who is an award-winning journalist at the Canadian Broadcasting Corp. and has taught data journalism at a number of educational institutions, there is a need to expand data journalism training at the public broadcaster to all journalists in order to "normalize" data skills. He describes data journalism as part of journalism's future, because it takes journalists "beyond the anecdote."

> I like to say anecdotes are nice, they can lead to wonderful stories, but they can be tyrannical and we become too dependent upon them for too many of our stories. It allows the powerful politicians to say, "well that's only an anecdote." What data allows you to do is it allows you to say "no, that's not an anecdote, that's actually a trend based on your own data."
>
> (McKie, 2018)

His approach is to train producers, reporters and assignment editors in order to "increase their sensitivities about data . . . and teach them some of these basic skills" (McKie, 2018).

The argument for increased training dovetails with research on professional development from Webster-Wright (2009), who argues that skill development is increasingly considered a necessity in a technological environment of rapid change. She studied a number of professions, including journalism as a social science, and found that, "across professions, from teaching and nursing, to engineering and architecture, there are increasing pressures towards the pursuit of more effective, efficient and evidence-based practices that deliver improved outcomes for clients whether they be students, patients or clients" (2009: p. 702). She defines generative and effective professional development as involving agency on the part of the professional, not as "part of a discourse that focuses on the professional as deficient and in need of developing and directing" but as about situating that professional, in our case journalists, as individuals "engaged in self-directed learning" (Webster-Wright, 2009: p. 713).

Journalism organizations – largely from studies in the United States – however, have historically offered limited professional development and insufficient mid-career training opportunities for journalists compared to other professions (Cleary, 2006; Knight Foundation, 2002; Webster-Wright, 2009). According to one of the few studies on professional development in journalism by Cleary (2006), who examined training in U.S. broadcast newsrooms, "most news organizations only spend a fraction of their budgets – if that – on professional development," identifying the amount as less than 1 per cent to 4 per cent of annual budgets (p. 254). She references a 2002 Knight Foundation report on newsroom training that journalism organizations were "lagging behind other knowledge-based companies and generally failing to meet professional development needs" and that training in the news business was "still too often thought of as an isolated frill" (Kees, 2002: p. 9). Cleary's study meanwhile found that while there was some professional development going on – largely in the form of "news topic-related seminars, followed by basic skills training" (p. 259) – producers did not believe there was "strong support from management for their professional development" and that it largely involved hiring consultants or outside trainers (p. 261).

Splendore et al. (2016) and Bradshaw (2018b), a prominent online U.K. journalist and journalism instructor, explore emerging self-directed forms of professional training in data journalism education, finding various approaches with the purpose and length of the training having an impact on the nature of students and their learning outcomes. They (Splendore et al., 2016) find that universities tend to offer a more "holistic approach" to data journalism education, while training programs are focused on skill development (p. 145). Bradshaw distinguishes between fast courses and slow courses as less about length and more about the nature of the content and approach. He defines fast teaching as "one-off classes and undergraduate modules involving data journalism" focused on "problem solving" (p. 64), compared to slow teaching that involves "a growing number of postgraduate courses which specifically focus on data or interactive/online journalism skills, alongside an increasing demand in the industry for journalism graduates with advanced data journalism skills" (p. 59). That both identify skill development as in high demand in self-directed studies reflect Heravi's (2018) finding that while the data journalism community is highly educated globally, its disciplinary expertise originates from communications and journalism-related degrees, rather than data and computer sciences.

In summary, there are a growing number of studies that assess data journalism education globally. Course learning outcomes largely focus on developing professional data journalism expertise through a focus on newsmaking processes and products, as well as traditional journalism ideologies that include teaching students to approach data as instrumental to uncovering a story (Borges-Rey, 2017; Parasie & Dagiral, 2013). There is a general orientation to entry-level courses, increasing opportunities for professional development and no significant reference to audiences, despite an active vision of journalism's multiple publics informing one of Coddington's (2019) four ways of assessing journalistic forms and practices in this domain. That the courses tend to prioritize processes and products reflects scholarly typologies of data journalism (Coddington, 2019), as well as approaches to journalism education more generally that have prioritized in situ training and professional practice oriented around form and specific genres (Young & Giltrow, 2015).

Drawing from genre theory, these findings suggest that educators understand the genre of data journalism as a recurrence of a recognizable form of journalism (Young & Giltrow, 2015). These forms – CAR, data stories, data visualizations – are consistent with journalism education's historical focus on forms considered industry relevant and economically viable and therefore a curricular priority. In this light, data journalism education in these studies is largely an expansion of traditional professional journalism expertise. However there is some evidence of network thinking and big data largely, although not exclusively, in collaboration-fueled experimentation in schools teaching across disciplines, explicitly connecting data journalism with other domains and epistemologies (Berret & Phillips, 2016; Royal, 2017). As a result, studies of course syllabi in numerous countries globally suggest that data journalism training is more aligned with educating students and professionals to be newshounds within traditional journalism norms, practices and mindsets than techies (Borges-Rey, 2017).

Data visualization for journalists

An example of a computer science-journalism collaboration that exemplifies the experimentation going on in Canadian journalism education involves a course one of us audited in Data Visualization for Journalists led by Tamara Munzner, a computer scientist and expert in information visualization, at the UBC School of Journalism in 2016, and co-taught by Caitlin Havlik, a data journalist at a Vancouver-based start-up. The course was a 1.5 credit data visualization module – half the size of a traditional course at the University of British Columbia School of Journalism. It was clear on the first day that the module was differently configured from other professional journalism courses at the school where we have both taught for almost 30 years combined.

In the first lecture, Munzner introduced novel ways of knowing and requisite expertise in two different domains: methods and audiences. She described information visualization as a field that draws from a variety of disciplines and methods ranging from anthropology/ethnography to design, computer science and cognitive psychology. She went on to talk about the limits of information visualization, identifying computational, human and display limits, and moving on to itemize how each discipline and/or method was relevant at various stages of the information visualization process with the caveats that "validation is difficult" and there are "different ways to get it wrong at each level" (Munzner, 2016).

Traditional journalism and journalism education does tend not to address core methodological limitations with respect to the journalist's ability to make truth claims, and how much of journalism's traditional method is dependent on interpretation. Her approach supported a transparent and complicated articulation of ways of knowing relative to method and a process to try to make valid and reliable knowledge claims in InfoVis (Broersma, 2010b; Callison & Young, forthcoming). By contrast, Bradshaw (2018b) articulates a more traditional approach to journalism education that locates a core expertise in data journalism in soft skills: "the real data journalism skill is to get better and better at learning new things – and to always be curious" (p. 61).

Second, Munzner incorporated the audience – in her domain "target users" – as central elements of the information visualization process, suggesting a before and after approach to assess need and "measure adoption" (Munzner, 2016). Her acknowledgment of the need for knowledge about and engagement with the audience reflects a networked understanding of the current socio-technical landscape as compared to the syllabi referenced in studies of data journalism education that prioritized form over audiences (Coddington, 2019). According to prominent audience scholar Sonia Livingstone (2014),

> should you be used to regarding the producer as more important than the consumer, the text more subtle than its various actualizations by readers, or the technology more fascinating than its uses, then I hope to persuade you that the study of media, communication and information technologies should always address the activities of users in context.
> (p. 241)

Conclusion

Lewis and Westlund's (2014) approach to understanding the integration of big data in journalism as based on four areas – "journalism's ways of knowing [epistemology] and doing [expertise], as well as its negotiation of value [economics] and values [ethics]" – is useful to think through the impact of data journalism on journalism education (p. 15). From a survey of studies of data journalism curricula globally, data journalism education is growing in prevalence, and largely evolving along traditional ways of journalism knowing and expertise as about form and the capacity to produce data journalism in certain technical and media political economic contexts. Bradshaw sums up the focus well when he suggests: "The challenge for a university seeking to offer data journalism education is this: how do you develop both editorial and technical skills in data journalism graduates" (Bradshaw, 2018a).

While the majority of studies show data journalism education as conforming to existing journalism education approaches from a *newshound* perspective, there is evidence of interdisciplinary collaborations that are incorporating ways of knowing and expertise aligned with a techie approach. More broadly, we suggest that the proliferation of data journalism education is testament to the fact that data journalism and the technologies associated with it, while still contested, are "settling into some comfortable frame of understanding" within the profession, since its incursion into the journalism lexicon and most recent rebranding and novel emergence of their professional identity[4] (Gillespie, Boczkowski & Foot, 2014: p. 13).

That the form is associated with newshound epistemologies we posit could be more a function of the power of journalism norms and the stabilizing and legitimizing role that form and style play to validate journalism's performative power to truth tell at a time of multiple field crises as referenced in Chapter 3 than resistance to technological ways of knowing and expertise (Broersma, 2010a). It is also consistent with journalism education's focus on form and genre as a proven orientation and way to classify journalism education, as well as the often implicit ways that professional journalism education has unfolded to the detriment of critical engagement with core norms and practices (Young & Giltrow, 2015). Finally, there is a surge of professional development with respect to data journalism education, which suggests these journalists are engaging in more self-directed learning. This approach is a departure from the past, and suggests a need for future research on the demand and effects of increasing self-directed learning in journalism more broadly.

Notes

1 They define this category as "including understanding sampling techniques and concepts of such as descriptive and predictive statistics, significance and error margins" (p. 137).
2 Other studies have found a gap in the number of trained data journalism instructors. In the United States, Berret and Phillips (2016) discovered that "many journalism programs do not have a faculty member skilled in data journalism" (p. 9).
3 Interdisciplinarity in data journalism education is not without its challenges as identified by Royal (2017) and Zhu and Du (2018). Zhu and Du (2018) explore the opportunities and challenges of interdisciplinary data education initiatives

when they examine the impact of learners' backgrounds in two programs in Hong Kong. They find students with a science background or science majors have advantages over journalism majors in learning outcomes. They speculate that the cause may be related to the "conceptual and cultural distance" between STEM and social sciences. Specifically they "found that a lack of prior knowledge, time and support in practice constrained interdisciplinary learning activities" with STEM majors gaining the upper hand because they have been exposed to more complex knowledge systems "behind visible scenes" (p. 30).

4 Bounegru (2012) in *The Data Journalism Handbook* indicates the first international data journalism conference in 2010 that she co-organized marks the period when the term data journalist started to emerge prominently.

References

Becker, L., Tudor, V., Mace, N., & Apperson, M. (2004) *Midcareer Training of Journalists: Evaluating Its Impact on Journalistic Work.* Porto Alegre, Brazil: Professional Education Section of the International Association for Media and Communication Research.

Berret, C., & Phillips, C. (2016) *Teaching Data and Computational Journalism.* Tow Center for Digital Journalism, Columbia Journalism School.

Bounegru, L. (2012) Data journalism in perspective. In: Gray, J., Bounegru, L., & Chambers, L. (eds.). *The Data Journalism Handbook.* Cambridge: O'Reilly. Available from: http://datajournalismhandbook.org/1.0/en/introduction_4.html

Borges-Rey, E. (2017) Towards an epistemology of data journalism in the devolved nations of the United Kingdom: Changes and continuities in materiality, performativity and reflexivity. *Journalism.* 1–18. DOI: 10.1177/1464884917693864

Bradshaw, P. (2018a) Designing data journalism courses: Reflections on a decade of teaching. *Online Journalism Blog*, June 21. Available from: https://onlinejournalismblog.com/2018/06/21/designing-data-journalism-courses-reflections-on-a-decade-of-teaching/ [Accessed 16 July 2018].

Bradshaw, P. (2018b) Data journalism teaching, fast and slow. *Asia Pacific Media Educator.* 28(1), 55–66. DOI: 10.1177/1326365X18769395

Brehmer, M., Ingram, S., Stray, J., & Munzner, T. (2014) Overview: The design, adoption, and analysis of a visual document mining tool for investigative journalists. *IEEE Transactions on Visualization and Computer Graphics (TVCG).* 20(12), 2271–2280. Proceedings of IEEE Conference on Information Visualization (InfoVis), Paris, France.

Broersma, M. (2010a) Journalism as performative discourse: The importance of form and style in journalism. In: Rupar, V. (ed.). *Journalism and Meaning-Making: Reading the Newspaper.* Cresskill, NJ: Hampton Press, pp. 15–35.

Broersma, M. (2010b) The unbearable limitations of journalism: On press critique and journalism's claim to truth. *The International Communication Gazette.* 72(1), 21–33.

Callison, C., & Young, M. L. (forthcoming) *The View from Somewhere: The Limits of Journalism.* New York: Oxford University Press.

Cleary, J. (2006) From the classroom to the newsroom: Professional development in broadcast journalism. *Journalism & Mass Communication Educator*, September, 254–266. https://doi.org/10.1177%2F107769580606100304

Coddington, M. (2015) Clarifying journalism's quantitative turn: A typology for evaluating data journalism, computational journalism, and computer-assisted reporting. *Digital Journalism*. 3(3), 331–348.

Coddington, M. (2019) Defining and mapping data journalism and computational journalism: A review of typologies and themes. In: Eldridge, S., II, & Franklin, B. (eds.). *The Routledge Handbook of Developments in Digital Journalism Studies*. Abingdon: Routledge.

Cohen, S., Hamilton, J., & Turner, F. (2011) Computational journalism. *Communications of the ACM*. 54(10), 66–71. DOI: 10.1145/2001269.2001288. Available from: https://cacm.acm.org/magazines/2011/10/131400-computational-journalism/fulltext

Davies, K., & Cullen, T. (2016) Data journalism classes in Australian universities: Educators describe progress to date. *Asia Pacific Media Educator*. 26(2), 132–147. DOI: 10.1177/1326365X16668969

Diakopolous, N. (2011) *A Functional Roadmap for Innovation in Computational Journalism*. Available from: www.nickdiakopoulos.com/2011/04/22/a-functional-roadmap-for-innovation-in-computational-journalism/

Gillespie, T., Boczkowski, P., & Foot, K. (2014) Introduction. In: Gillespie, T., Boczkowski, P., & Foot, K. (eds.). *Media Technologies: Essays on Communication, Materiality and Society*. Cambridge, MA: MIT Press.

Green, S. (2018) When the numbers don't add up: Accommodating data journalism in a compact journalism programme. *Asia Pacific Media Educator*. 28(1), 78–90.

Heravi, B. (2018) 3Ws of data journalism education. *Journalism Practice*. https://doi.org/10.1080/17512786.2018.1463167

Hewett, J. (2017) Collaborative learning: From CAR to data journalism and Hacks/Hackers. In: Mair, J., Keeble, R. L., Lucero, M., & Moore, M. (eds.). *Data Journalism: Past, Present and Future*. Bury St Edmunds: Abramis, pp. 5–22.

Howard, A. B. (2014) *The Art and Science of Data-Driven Journalism*. Tow Center for Digital Journalism, Columbia Journalism School.

Kees, B. (2002) Newsroom training: Where's the investment. *A Study for the Council of Presidents of National Journalism Organizations*. Knight Foundation Report, October 18. Available from: https://knightfoundation.org/reports/newsroom-training-wheres-investment [Accessed 15 July 2018].

Knight Foundation. (2002) *No. 1 Complaint of U.S. Journalists Is Lack of Training, New National Survey Says*. Available from: https://knightfoundation.org/press/releases/no-1-complaint-of-us-journalists-is-lack-of [Accessed 26 September 2018].

Leask, J. L. (2017) *Data Journalism in Canada: Challenges and Opportunities*. (Unpublished masters thesis). University of Alberta, Edmonton, AB, Canada.

Lewis, S., & Westlund, O. (2015) Big data and journalism: Epistemology, Expertise, Economics and Ethics. *Digital Journalism*, 3(3), 447–466. DOI: 10.1080/21670811.2014.976418

Livingstone, S. (2014) Identifying the interests of digital users as audiences, consumers, workers, and publics. In: Gillespie, T., Bozckowski, P., & Foot, K. (eds.). *Media Technologies: Essays on Communication, Materiality, and Society*. Cambridge: MIT Press, pp. 241–250.

McKie, D. Journalist (Personal communication, 8 June 2018).

Munzner, T. (2016) *Visualization for Journalists*. University of British Columbia Course, September. Available from: www.cs.ubc.ca/~tmm/

Parasie, S., & Dagiral, E. (2013) Data-driven journalism and the public good: 'Computer-assisted-reporters' and 'programmer-journalists' in Chicago. *New Media & Society*. 15(6), 853–871.

Royal, C. (2017) Coding the curriculum: Journalism education for the digital age. In: Goodman, R. S., & Steyn, E. (eds.). *Global Journalism Education in the 21st Century: Challenges and Innovations*. Austin, TX: Knight Center for Journalism in the Americas, University of Texas.

Splendore, S., Di Salvo, P., Eberwein, T., Groenhart, H., Kus, M., & Porlezza, C. (2016) Educational strategies in data journalism: A comparative study of Six European countries. *Journalism*. 17(1), 138–152. DOI: 10.1177/1464884915612683

Webster-Wright, A. (2009) Reframing professional development through understanding authentic professional learning. *Review of Educational Research*. 79(2), 702–739.

Wing, J. M. (2006) Computational thinking. *Communications of the ACM*, March, 49(3), 33–35.

Wosen, J. (2016) Seeing is believing: Tamara Munzner's keynote on visualization and journalism. *Medium*, October. Available from: https://medium.com/@StanfordJournalism/seeing-is-believing-tamara-munzners-keynote-on-visualization-and-journalism-e9ed1808e629 [Accessed 10 July 2018].

Young, M. L., & Giltrow, J. (2015) A mobile responsive expertise: Thinking more productively and generatively about journalism education. In: Allen, G., Craft, S., Waddell, C., & Young, M. L. (eds.). *Toward 2020: New Directions in Journalism Education*. Toronto: Ryerson Journalism Research Centre (online publication), pp. 46–63.

Zhu, L., & Du, Y. R. (2018) Interdisciplinary learning in journalism: A Hong Kong study of data journalism education. *Asia Pacific Educator*. 28(1), 16–37.

6 Conclusion

Almost a decade ago, Canada was lauded as leading the way in data journalism. In a 2010 article in the *Guardian*, well-known U.K. data journalist and columnist Simon Rogers argued Canada was becoming a data journalism hub as a result of its combination of journalistic expertise and open data. Rogers talked of a "new breed" of journalists, highlighting the work of a number of respected data journalists across the country. Among them was Patrick Cain, who was using data to produce maps of Toronto concerns and stories. Referencing Cain's journalism, Rogers wrote: "Imagine if you took the historic records of everyone who died in the first world war. Then you matched them to one area to see how it had been affected. Or if you wanted to see if one part of your city had an epidemic of bedbugs. Or if you wanted to find out where the most guns are" (2010: para.1). For Rogers, such work was "the pinnacle of what data journalism is supposed to be about. And, if you're looking for innovative data journalism, vast open data resources and the latest open data apps, Canada is a good place to start" (2010: para.3).

His argument that the interrelationships between access to information through open data initiatives and journalistic expertise have made Canada a data "powerhouse" touches on some of the themes that we explore throughout this book. Three years after Rogers wrote his column, we first set out to examine what data journalism, a subspecialty of journalism with its own forms and processes, could tell us about organizational change, technology, expertise and power in journalism (Usher, 2016). We started in the U.S., through an initial study of data journalism at the *Los Angeles Times* (Young & Hermida, 2015). We found an uneven adaptation of data and computational journalism in a single journalistic site. The integration process was affected by shifting definitions of news, newer expertise and identities including skills and competencies in computational thinking, algorithmic technologies, and historic practices grounded in newsroom economics.

Our later research focused solely on Canada as a site of exploration using a multi methodological approach combining qualitative interviews and content analysis of data journalism awards entries from Canadian journalism organizations. Our interviews initially included almost the entire sample of Canadian data journalists in 2015 (Hermida & Young, 2017), with an update of a few key interviews in 2018. Our content analysis covered the period of 2012–2015 – beginning when data journalism became a separate and distinct award category. A data journalism series on unfounded rates of sexual assault in police departments across the country by Canada's largest national daily newspaper, examined in Chapter 3, was recognized in a number of journalism awards in 2017.

Canada serves as our main site of study for this book because of its distinct media system and our years of research. It includes a small number of well-funded news organizations making international contributions to data journalism (which is where much of the research has focused on in this field. See, for example, Tandoc & Oh, 2017). Canada also has a prominent public service broadcaster, which operates in a number of languages (including eight Indigenous languages in CBC North, French and English), and largely small and mid-sized journalism organizations (Shade, 2005) with various national and regional commitments to open data (for a critique, see Marczak & Sieber, 2018). With respect to ownership, Canada has been characterized by numerous scholars as an example of a country with a highly concentrated journalism industry (Picard, 2016). For example, Winseck noted how the *Toronto Star* was the only newspaper that did not endorse Conservative party candidate Stephen Harper for prime minister. "In other words, 95% of editorial opinion expressed plunked for Steven Harper – roughly three times his standing in opinion polls at the time and the results of the prior election" (Winseck, 2016a: para.28).

Moreover, Canadian media are facing decline at the local level similar to other mature media systems, with the loss of 248 local news outlets between 2008 and 2018 (Lindgren & Corbett, 2018). In this context, a 2017 report on the state of the media in Canada led by journalism insiders raised an alarm about the "waning status of traditional journalism" (Public Policy Forum, 2017: p. 11). According to the report, "once indispensable agencies of information, the 20th-century news media are less and less prominent, except to provide grist for a public conversation they no longer control" (Public Policy Forum, 2017: p. 17). As part of a number of recommendations, the report later mentioned the need for funding for "the use of data and evidence in journalism" as it is linked to excellence in civic journalism (Public Policy Forum, 2017: p. 88).

We find data journalists at the coalface of a number of crises and changes in journalism related to competition from platforms, active audiences and concerns about legitimacy in addition to a growing technoculture in journalism more generally (Lewis & Usher, 2013). Our narrow window of research comes at a time that data journalism is being both rebranded and emerging in newer forms, processes and identities. Combined with the specific national context of English language Canadian media, the time is ripe to think about larger questions of order and change in the field of journalism in one country. Peters and Broersma have suggested that the way journalism plays with "conventions of storytelling and platforms upon which they are told" are "central to journalism's strategies of adaptation in this changing context and impacts on the way that information is communicated and flows" (Peters & Broersma, 2014: p. xi). In this book, we add occupational identities as Usher (2016) has characterized this growing domain of journalism as a subspecialty.

We draw from organizational and institutional theory along with our past location within media hybridity and STS to make some early inferences about what is happening in the larger field in one country. We take a generative view of the field of journalism as a domain characterized by "conflict and change as far more common than the prevailing view of settled fields" (Fligstein & McAdam, 2011: p. 5). Given the focus of the series in which this book is a part, this approach allows us to decenter the ubiquitous use of the term disruption and question its impact on scholarship through examining a specific set of organizational actors – data journalists (Lawrence & Suddaby, 2006).

This approach enables us to critically engage with the ways that disruption has been used rhetorically to describe a field that now contains almost 20 years of digitalization, digital experiences, ways of being and doing journalism. It also recognizes the contributions that have been made to understanding disruptive innovations in journalism at the economic and firm level (Christensen, Skok & Allworth, 2012). Such an approach considers conflict as more constant and generative for adaptation and culture. It moves beyond a focus on technological adaption as a main conflict or problem to solve, instead shifting to the actions of groups of actors including technologies and data as material actors (see Chapter 4 on materiality) and their roles in transforming and maintaining fields (Fligstein & McAdam, 2011; Lawrence & Suddaby, 2006).[1] We have come to this constellation of approaches as we have observed data journalism expertise gathering momentum and growing profile internal and external to journalism over our years of study.

A data journalism divide?

Throughout the book, we have charted how the growth of subspeciality of journalism – the data journalist – has played out in different institutional contexts in Canada. We find data journalists increasingly able to promote their own professional interests, identity and community of practice at well-resourced media organizations, as freelance actors, educators and as non-human actors and technological applications such as Google Maps. The most prominent site of this trend was at the country's largest national newspaper, the *Globe and Mail*. Over the course of four years, a small interactive team grew to a Visual Journalism team with 34 reporters, analysts and editors listed on the website as of July 2018, encompassing formerly distinct professional identities such as graphics. It is the largest team of its kind in Canada. A data journalism series supported by this team has become a prominent reference point for excellence in journalism in English Canada. Signs of the increased strategic and professional identity of data journalists are also evident in the Canadian Broadcasting Corporation, which has added to a central programming team by hiring designated data journalists in four regional newsrooms. We suggest these gains are the result of data journalists able to leverage crises over legitimacy and audiences in the context of a growing technoculture in journalism to advance their professional identities and interests.

We find the degree of power and agency of these actors however still tempered by the economic, cultural and organizational norms and practices, within the overall framework of what Chadwick describes as the "evolving interrelationships among older and newer media logics" (2013: p. 3). Our work on the landscape in Canada serves as a further illustration of the stratification of data journalism identified in other national studies. Similar to our past research, we find an unevenness of results with data journalists emerging as a powerful identity in the most well-funded journalism organizations to the extent that the size of the team at Canada's largest national newspaper, the *Globe and Mail*, is equal or larger than the largest identified in global studies. In fact, over the course of our research, the allocation of significant resources and priority given to data-driven journalism increased at the legacy print organization and at the public broadcaster. Beyond what may be seen as elite media in Canada, support for data journalism was either consistent with buttressing a transition to digital, or there was a laissez-faire attitude towards individual journalists with experience and a track record in this domain.

Thus, despite excitement in the industry and a flurry of attention by scholars, we find the data journalist affected by the increasing precarity of journalism (Deuze, 2018; Picard, 2016). Canada as we mention in Chapter 1 has seen a relative decline in the number of journalists compared to the rest of the workplace of 20 per cent since 2001. During the course of our study of data journalists in Canada, a number of interviewees were reassigned, changed employers or left the profession. The precarity of data journalism emerges in a broad range of other national studies, reflecting a lack of people, skills and technologies. In their 2015 paper, Fink and Anderson sounded the alarm that "if the gap between data journalism resources is as wide as our preliminary research suggests, this would add to an already considerable list of concerns about the future of newspapers in all but the largest metropolitan areas in the United States" (2015: p. 480). A similar regional divide exists in the U.K. with Borges-Rey noting that "regional data journalism – with a few exceptions such as the detail, Trinity Mirror, and BBC Scotland – tends to be strongly limited by internal organizational and editorial pressures and by scarce human and material resources" (2016: p. 839). Some have taken this further to suggest that this form of journalism is creating "data elites" (Dickinson, 2014: p. 122), with Felle noting that the U.K. "media outlets with the heaviest investment in and strongest record of data journalism so far are among the least popular titles that serve elite niche audiences, rather than those with lower socio-economic status" (2016: p. 88).

The technological imagination of data journalism

The emergent relations in data journalism are happening within a broader technological context, hence our attention to how materiality and its intersection with journalistic ways of knowing and ways of doing. We suggest this is an underdeveloped area of study, given the impact of the objects of data journalism, from the data sets to the tools and platforms for producing the work itself. An examination of the tools of data journalism contributes to understanding how the practice has evolved. We found that technology aligns with the three quantitative forms of journalism detailed in Coddington's typology (2015, 2019). Excel was closely associated with Computer-Assisted Reporting, mapping with data journalism and algorithmic methods with computational journalism.

As part of the growth in data journalism charted in our research, we find older forms of journalism expertise such as graphics and photography becoming merged under the category of data journalist such as maps and charts. These two forms of data representation and visualization are increasingly prevalent across media. One of our studies found maps used in 14 out of 26 projects our study (Young, Hermida & Fulda, 2018). The forms of data journalism deserve greater scrutiny. As D'Ignazio argues, "even when we rationally know that data visualizations do not represent 'the whole world,' we forget that fact and accept charts as facts because they are generalized, scientific and seem to present an expert, neutral point of view" (2017: para.1). Such a critique is applicable to mapping, which has become one of the most visible aspects of data journalism. Critical cartographers have linked maps to representations of power, ideology and bias (see for example, Harley, 1989). What is included and excluded on a map "surfaces the problem of knowledge in an inescapable fashion as do symbolization, generalization and classification" (Wood & Krygier, 2009: p. 344).

Indeed, as we discuss in Chapter 4, some emerging technologies for data analysis and visualization such as Google Maps are double-edged. They present a closed black box for journalism while simultaneously supporting newer graphic/visualization forms and affecting practice through the standards, values and user possibilities embedded in the software (Ananny, 2016; Young, Hermida & Fulda, 2018). Here there is unevenness marked by the materiality of technology with smaller and more financially constrained organizations using out of the box solutions. The widespread use and reliance on free, third-party cartographic tools such as Google Maps, enable resource-poor newsrooms to create newer graphical and interactive forms of journalism. Simultaneously, though, they serve to define and confine practice due to embedded standards, values and functionality. As a result, the ability of data journalists to advance newer methods and forms may be undercut by the accessibility of free tools and by a lack of institutional investment in technologies and training. Other software tools/environments such as R and in-house solutions can facilitate a greater ability to experiment with methods, form and journalistic authority, opening up journalism and news to norms, processes and values from other disciplines and epistemologies. Well-funded organizations, such as the *Globe*, are able to create in-house options in its visual journalism unit, moving to AI and computational journalism expertise to create basic charts. This move we suggest is part of an already identified trend in labor specialization in journalism that scholars such as Berry (1994) have identified in his study of the *London Free Press* and USA Today as news organizations place value on specific kinds of expertise in the process of rationalization.

Similarly, the increasing availability of some public open data in Canada is both generative in that it enables journalists to surface more news stories and constrictive as available data sets funnel reporting towards certain types of topics and issues (Hamilton, 2006; Janssen, Charalabidis & Zuiderwijk, 2012). As we've explored in Chapter 4, there is a significant dependence of data derived from public records or easily accessible information in data journalism projects (Loosen, Reimer & De Silva-Schmidt, 2017; Tabary, Provost & Trottier, 2016; Young, Hermida & Fulda, 2018). Studies show an over-representation of data stories on public services at the expense of stories on the corporate world, which suggests an incongruence with the investigative claims that tend to be associated with data journalism (Gray, Bounegru & Chambers, 2012; Howard, 2014).

Since Canada is our site of study, there is an additional factor to consider. It is unclear how far the use of public data sets is due to the challenges around the freedom of information (FOI) process in Canada, or how far this may be the case in other countries. Canada has been ranked top alongside the U.K. for open data (World Wide Web Foundation, 2018), but ranked 56th globally in terms of its access to information provisions (Centre for Law and Democracy, 2018). A review of Canada's FOI practices by the Office of the Information Minister of Canada headed by Commissioner Suzanne Legault into access of information suggested there was a need at the highest levels for a "concomitant change in institutional culture from secrecy to openness, from delay to timeliness" (2015: p. 4). The challenges in accessing information could be a contributory factor to the common use of public data sets in Canada, as a consequence influence what is reported. Considering the data set as an object of journalism, then, provides a lens to scope out how technology interacts with journalistic epistemology and practice.

Maintaining a fluid field

Papacharissi (2015) has argued that digital technologies have enabled and co-produced a flowering of journalisms. Our contribution is to assess and understand stability and change within a subspecialty of journalism in a specific national context. Data journalism is one articulation of a multiverse of journalisms, but one that we suggest is increasing its authority through the "purposive action" of its professional group within Canada (Lawrence & Suddaby, 2006: p. 215). The data journalist as an occupational subspeciality can be seen to address acutely felt issues of trust and credibility in the news media, particularly at a time of multiple crises in journalism. By turning to data to go beyond the anecdotal, data journalists seek to make claims about certainty, facts and truth (Anderson, 2018).

We see signs of settling in this subspeciality as forms and practices coalesce around shared notions of data journalism even while precise definitions remain fuzzy. Our research supports Lowrey's contention that "over time innovative news forms and practices emerge in *variation*, flock together in a *selection* process, stabilize, and then demonstrate *retention*" (2012: p. 216, italics in original). We suggest that this process is in part successful because it is participating in the construction and maintenance of journalism authority in the context of multiple crises. Here, we find data journalists able to claim authority largely within a newshound framework (Borges-Rey, 2017), which connects to established investigative and watchdog functions of journalism and traces its genealogy to precision journalism and computer-assisted reporting. Similarly, the prevalence of maps and charts, together with heavy dependence on public data, signal how certain long-standing approaches to data are being specialized, institutionalized, routinized and incorporating other historic journalism identities in newsrooms and within journalism education.

Alongside maintenance, there are signs of regeneration through emergent ways of doing and knowing. Across the media landscape, we see increasing leanings towards sociological collaboration over competition, as normative poles that orient the field (Boyles & Meyer, 2016; Lewis & Usher, 2014; Sambrook, 2018). Here, we find a shared commitment to transparency and collaboration, as well as an increasing role for professional development. As part of this reorientation of the field, we find elements of newer kinds of interdependencies within journalism in Canada such as collaborations across media. Such interdependencies extend beyond Canada. As one example, four of the six finalists in the 2017 and 2018 Online Journalism Award for investigative data journalism were collaborations between media organizations in the U.S.

Such collaboration exists at an individual level too. We found evidence of informal training networks, with support groups on the Slack team messaging platform to support expertise and professional development in this space. The willingness to share resources is partly caused by necessity, given a lack of institutional backing, training and/or resources at many medium and smaller sized news organizations. But it also reflects a shared culture and an ideology of collaboration drawing from the field of programming and coding (Lewis & Usher, 2013; Lewis & Zamith, 2017). In closing, as institutional entrepreneurs and strategic actors at the coalface of a number of crises, data journalists are actively contributing to the discursive and technical construction of what journalism can and should do 20 years after digitalization.

Note

1 See Winseck (2016b: p. 492) for an important discussion of the power of larger structures: "If media history tells us anything, it is that once the structures of a new medium are cemented into place they stay that way for a long time. Indeed, the structure of the industrial media age set down in the late 19th and early 20th centuries has only begun to give way to the network media ecology of the 21st century in the past decade with no small amount of resistance from entrenched interests all along the line."

References

Ananny, M. (2016) Toward an ethics of algorithms: Convening, observation, probability, and timeliness. *Science, Technology, & Human Values*. 41(1), 93–117.

Anderson, C. (2018) *Apostles of Certainty: Data Journalism and the Politics of Doubt*. Oxford: Oxford University Press.

Berry, S. (1994) USA Today, the *London Free Press*, and the rationalization of the North American newspaper industry. *Canadian Journal of Communication*. 19(2).

Borges-Rey, E. (2016) Unravelling data journalism: A study of data journalism practice in British newsrooms. *Journalism Practice*. 10(7), 833–843.
Borges-Rey, E. (2017) Towards an epistemology of data journalism in the devolved nations of the United Kingdom: Changes and continuities in materiality, performativity and reflexivity. *Journalism*. [Preprint]. https://doi.org/10.1177/1464884917693864 [Accessed 15 April 2018].
Boyles, J. L., & Meyer, E. (2016) Letting the data speak: Role perceptions of data journalists in fostering democratic conversation. *Digital Journalism*. 4(7), 944–954.
Centre for Law and Democracy. (2018) *The RTI Rating*. Available from: www.rti-rating.org/country-data/ [Accessed 28 September 2018].
Chadwick, A. (2013) *The Hybrid Media System: Politics and Power*. Oxford: Oxford University Press.
Christensen, C. M., Skok, D., & Allworth, J. (2012) Breaking news: Mastering the art of disruptive innovation in journalism. *Nieman Reports*. 66(3), 6–20.
Coddington, M. (2015) Clarifying journalism's quantitative turn: A typology for evaluating data journalism, computational journalism, and computer-assisted reporting. *Digital Journalism*. 3(3), 331–348.
Coddington, M. (2019) Defining and mapping data journalism and computational journalism: A review of typologies and themes. In: Eldridge, S., II, & Franklin, B. (eds.). *The Routledge Handbook of Developments in Digital Journalism Studies*. Abingdon: Routledge.
Deuze, M. (2018) *Beyond Journalism: Entrepreneurial Journalism Around the World*. Available from: https://riuma.uma.es/xmlui/handle/10630/15049 [Accessed 8 September 2018].
Dickinson, A. (2014) Does data journalism help democracy? In: Mair, J., & Keeble, R. (eds.). *Data Journalism: Mapping the Future*. Bury St Edmunds: Abramis, pp. 91–98.
D'Ignazio, C. (2017) What would feminist data visualization look like? *Medium*. Available from: https://medium.com/@kanarinka/what-would-feminist-data-visualization-look-like-aa3f8fc7f96c [Accessed 4 September 2018].
Felle, T. (2016) Digital watchdogs? Data reporting and the news media's traditional 'fourth estate' function. *Journalism*. 17(1), 85–96.
Fink, K., & Anderson, C. W. (2015) Data journalism in the United States: Beyond the 'usual suspects'. *Journalism Studies*. 6(4), 467–481.
Fligstein, N., & McAdam, D. (2011) Toward a general theory of strategic action fields. *Sociological Theory*. 29(1), 1–26.
Gray, J., Bounegru, L., & Chambers, L. (2012) *The Data Journalism Handbook*. Sebastopol, CA: O'Reilly Media.
Hamilton, J. (2006) *All the News That's Fit to Sell: How the Market Transforms Information into News*. Princeton, NJ: Princeton University Press.
Harley, J. B. (1989) Deconstructing the map. *Cartographica: The International Journal for Geographic Information and Geovisualization*. 26(2), 1–20.
Hermida, A., & Young, M. L. (2017) Finding the data unicorn: A hierarchy of hybridity in data and computational journalism. *Digital Journalism*. 5(2), 159–176.

Howard, A. B. (2014) The art and science a-driven journalism. *Tow Center for Journalism White Paper*. Available from: https://academiccommons.columbia.edu/catalog/ac:zcrjdfn317

Janssen, M., Charalabidis, Y., & Zuiderwijk, A. (2012) Benefits, adoption barriers and myths of open data and open government. *Information Systems Management*. 29(4), 258–268.

Lawrence, T. B., & Suddaby, R. (2006) Institutions and institutional work. In: Clegg, S. R., Hardy, C., Lawrence, T. B., & Nord, W. R. (eds.) *Sage Handbook of Organization Studies*, 2nd Edition. London: Sage Publications, pp. 215–254.

Legault, S. (2015) Striking the right balance for transparency. *Office of the Information Commissioner of Canada*. Available from: www.ci-oic.gc.ca/eng/rapport-%20de%20modernisation-modernization-report.aspx [Accessed 3 September 2018].

Lewis, S. C., & Usher, N. (2013) Open source and journalism: Toward new frameworks for imagining news innovation. *Media, Culture & Society*. 35(5), 602–619.

Lewis, S. C., & Usher, N. (2014) Code, collaboration, and the future of journalism: A case study of the Hacks/Hackers global network. *Digital Journalism*. 2(3), 383–393.

Lewis, S. C., & Zamith, R. (2017) On the worlds of journalism. In: Boczkowski, P. J., & Anderson, C. W. (eds.), *Remaking the News: Essays on Technology and the Futures of Journalism Scholarship in the Digital Age*. Cambridge, MA: MIT Press.

Lindgren, A., & Corbett, J. (2018) Local news map cata. *Local News Research Project*. Available from: http://localnewsresearchproject.ca/category/local-news-map-data [Accessed 27 August 2018].

Loosen, W., Reimer, J., & De Silva-Schmidt, F. (2017) Data-driven reporting: An on-going (r). evolution? An analysis of projects nominated for the Data Journalism Awards 2013–2016. *Journalism*. [Preprint]. https://doi.org/10.1177/1464884917735691 [Accessed 15 April 2018].

Lowrey, W. (2012) Journalism innovation and the ecology of news production: Institutional tendencies. *Journalism & Communication Monographs*. 14(4), 214–287.

Marczak, P., & Sieber, R. (2018) Linking legislative openness to open data in Canada. *The Canadian Geographer/Le Géographe canadien*. 62(2), 106–119.

Papacharissi, Z. (2015) Toward new journalism (s) affective news, hybridity, and liminal spaces. *Journalism Studies*. 16(1), 27–40.

Peters, C., & Broersma, M. (2014) Introduction: Retelling journalism: Conveying stories in a digital age. In: Broersma, M., & Peters, C. (eds.). *Retelling Journalism*. Walpole, MA: Peeters. Groningen Studies in Cultural Change, Vol. 49, pp. ix–xix.

Picard, R. (2016) Submission to the House of Commons Standing Committee on Canadian Heritage, Local Media Inquiry, Email Sent to Mary Lynn Young, October 1.

Public Policy Forum. (2017) *The Shattered Mirror: News, Democracy and Trust in the Digital Age*. Available from: https://shatteredmirror.ca/wpcontent/uploads/theShatteredMirror.pdf. [Accessed DATE].

Rogers, S. (2010) How Canada became an open data and data journalism powerhouse. *The Guardian*, November 9. Available from: www.theguardian.com/news/datablog/2010/nov/09/canada-open-data [Accessed 3 September 2018].

Sambrook, R. (2018) *Global Teamwork: The Rise of Collaboration in Investigative Journalism*. Oxford: Reuters Institute for the Study of Journalism.

Shade, L. R. (2005) Aspergate: Concentration, convergence, and censorship in Canadian media. In: Skinner, D., Compton, J. R., & Gasher, M. (eds.). *Converging Media, Diverging Politics: A Political Economy of News Media in the United States and Canada*. Lanham, MD: Lexington Books, pp. 101–106.

Tabary, C., Provost, A. M., & Trottier, A. (2016) Data journalism's actors, practices and skills: A case study from Quebec. *Journalism*. 17(1), 66–84.

Tandoc, E. C., Jr, & Oh, S. K. (2017) Small departures, big continuities? *Journalism Studies*. 1(1), 997–1015.

Usher, N. (2016) *Interactive Journalism: Hackers, Data, and Code*. Urbana, IL: University of Illinois Press.

Winseck, D. (2016a) Media and Internet concentration in Canada report 1984–2015. *Canadian Media Concentration Research Project*. Available from: www.cmcrp.org/media-and-internet-concentration-in-canada-report-1984-2015/ [Accessed 3 September 2018].

Winseck, D. (2016b) Media ownership and concentration in Canada. In Noam, E. M. (ed.). *Who Owns the World's Media? Media Concentration and Ownership Around the World*. Oxford: Oxford University Press, pp. 455–493.

Wood, D., & Krygier, J. (2009) Critical cartography. In: Kitchin, R., & Thrift, N. (eds.). *The International Encyclopedia of Human Geography*. New York and London: Elsevier, pp. 340–344.

World Wide Web Foundation. (2018) *Open Data Barometer*. Available from: https://opendatabarometer.org/doc/leadersEdition/ODB-leadersEdition-Report.pdf [Accessed 28 September 2018].

Young, M. L., & Hermida, A. (2015) From Mr. and Mrs. outlier to central tendencies: Computational journalism and crime reporting at the Los Angeles Times. *Digital Journalism*. 3(3), 381–397.

Young, M. L., Hermida, A., & Fulda, J. (2018) What makes for great data journalism? A content analysis of data journalism awards finalists 2012–2015. *Journalism Practice*. 12(1), 115–135.

Index